Canapés,
Hors D'Oeuvres
and Buffet Dishes

JANET LEFLER, *Department Head*

MILDRED RUPP, *Assistant Department Head*

FELICE CHIAPPERINI, *Instructor*

Hotel Technology,
New York City Community College

Appetizers Prepared and Photographed by

JANE AND HUBERT KRANTZ

AHRENS BOOK COMPANY, INC., NEW YORK

a division of HAYDEN PUBLISHING COMPANY, INC.

Master Chef Leopold Instructor
Leopold K. Schaeli, C.M.C.
7496 Pebble Lane
West Bloomfield, MI 48322
(313) 855-9259

Preface

FOOD and drink are the traditional courtesies extended to the guest on entrance by the thoughtful host and hostess. Whether in the home, at the restaurant table, or in a private dining room, the cocktail—to paraphrase the song—can't do without the food and certainly should not! It is no news to the professional that in this day of "on the rocks" drinking, the hors d'oeuvre should be introduced simultaneously with the cocktail.

A book on hors d'oeuvres needs no excuse, explanation, or reason for being. It affords the chef an opportunity to express himself. This expression is in the manner in which he combines his ingredients, and embellishes the dainties into tasty temptations.

The idea in this book may be considered for development as well as finished recipes. The practical chef will build—and building does not necessarily mean further elaboration. Simplification of recipe should follow both for the kitchen's sake as well as for public reaction, visually and in taste. While it is true that eye appeal is essential in any dish, this appeal should be supported by the ingredients and reaction on the taste buds when placed in the mouth.

One caution must be stressed by continual repetition, as both the kitchen and the dining room staffs tend to forget an important aspect of service: maintain warm and hot foods properly (not burned by heat under a chafing dish), and keep items destined for presentation at room temperature so they are not cold, soggy, nor tasting of the refrigerator. All this takes co-ordination between kitchen and dining room, and an evaluation of facilities within the establishment.

Trays unduly heaped with goodies, or those seriously depleted, turn appetites, no matter how elegant the individual dainty when it left the artist's hands. The executives of the culinary and the dining room departments are beseeched to co-ordinate and thus to maintain standards of high quality which mark the fine restaurant.

This book, written by three members of the staff of the Hotel Technology Department of the New York City Community College, reads for itself. It is precise, concise, and can be used as a manual or path upon which the chef can travel to places of his own choosing. It must be remembered that the authors of this book are dedicated to the culinary art and equally dedicated to the instruction of students and/or apprentices. The experienced practitioner can read this as a refresher or as a stimulant to the imagination.

The purpose of this book is to remind one and all of the great need to develop the interest of young men and women in the art of our industry. The word drudgery should be dropped from the lexicon as it applies to the kitchen; instead, those words should be substituted which create a picture of service to family and friends around a festive table, enjoying one of the pleasurable experiences in life—dining.

The young who pursue careers in the hotel or restaurant industry—those who are developing now and also the fully grown who have achieved careers of distinction—must remember that after us will follow other generations, all entitled to even better facilities for instruction than those we now possess. Our plea is that those who read these words not forget that many dedicated people performed yeoman service for our benefit. Those who read this must remember and help the ones who follow with money for facilities and time in which to give instruction with patience for the beginner.

Jerry Berns
"21" Club

DEDICATION

To: Louis Ploneis, executive chef, Twenty-One Club
Eugene Scanlan, executive chef, Waldorf Astoria
Albert Stockli, supervising chef, Restaurant Associates

We are proud to dedicate this book to three outstanding executive chefs who have four characteristics in common: rare and imaginative ability, an adventurous courage with new ideas in food preparation, warm genial personalities, and the desire and ability to train young men toward a future in the culinary arts.

The Authors

Contents

1. Introduction

TO assemble all known and available information on canapés and hors d'oeuvres would be an Herculean task. If such an encyclopedia of appetizers was produced, the fact would remain that there would be very little of startling originality. Somewhere, at some place, someone has in all probability produced a tasty tidbit which he fondly imagines to be his alone.

With no desire to disillusion these creative artists, it must be accepted that there is practically nothing edible that some chef, housewife, food editor, dietician, or catering manager hasn't dreamed up and arranged for display and gastronomic delight. Those in the know (foodwise), from thrifty housewife to cost-conscious chef, appreciate the wisdom of converting yesterday's leftovers into today's canapés and casseroles. This book is written with just such a thought in mind: To develop and utilize a basic list of items that can be changed with the whisk of a seasoning and garnished from an open-faced smear on a cracker to a delight to the eye as well as a whet to the appetite.

Items that may be refrigerated as well as those that may be frozen will be so indicated for greater convenience.

Today, merchandising has spread from cloaks-and-suits to cocktail lounges. Fortunately, from the food control point of view, the day of the old free-lunch saloon spread has long since given way to the daintier nibbles of peanuts, pretzels, and potato chips. More and more hot and cold canapés and hors d'oeuvres are sparking a heavier cocktail hour trade.

1

There are economic, geographic, and psychological reasons for the growing interest in finer foods served in more attractive settings. Cooking schools for both amateur and professional cooks are creating a revived respect for the culinary arts.

Catering houses from a one-man—or more often, a one-woman—operation to a large staffed, highly functional business are giving the public a taste of exotic foods in homes and halls.

The smart young marrieds have devised the "each bring a dish" dinner so that suburban kitchens throughout the country are aromatic bouquets of fine herbs as "specialties" become party necessities.

Cookbooks pour off the presses, and home kitchens as well as professional ones boast a well-stocked bookshelf as well as a pantry shelf.

Magazines print colorful and enticing food stories both in advertisements and editorial copy. These are aided and abetted by the daily and Sunday newspapers with full pages devoted to culinary delights.

Airline and steamship advertising has made millions of potential customers conscious of the lure of exotic foreign foods. Thanks to the kitchens where some of the finest national dishes of other countries are prepared and often glamorized, the Foreign Intrigue chapter in this book offers a wide variety of easily adaptable gems.

So the interest exists. The public who pays wants the best and the most exciting foods. It is our hope that this book will aid those who prepare and serve food to make ever greater profits with cocktail tidbits and buffet casseroles.

The Authors

2. Butters

BUTTERS are used as fillings, spreads, bases, and decorations. It is advisable to allow the creamery butter base to warm slightly at room temperature before attempting to incorporate the other ingredients into it. This makes a smoother, more equally flavored, and homogeneous paste which is essential in this type of work. The quantities and types of butters one may use are limited only by individual imagination.

It is advisable to use a high-speed mixer to break down the ingredients to be used with the butter. This eliminates the need of passing these ingredients through a fine sieve before incorporation. It must be remembered that a fine star tube pastry nozzle is quite important in the application of these butters, and one small "chunk" of an ingredient, not small enough to flow through the tube, can clog it, causing a great deal of inconvenience; hence the importance of the fine pureeing or sieving. (Lightly salted butter may be used, except when sweet butter is called for.)

Listed below you will find some of the more popular types.

1. **Lobster Butter**
   Puree 8 ozs. of cooked lobster trimmings and coral and blend smoothly with 8 ozs. of softened butter.

2. **Anchovy Butter**
   Puree 40 (approximately) anchovy filets and blend with 1 lb. of sweet butter.

3

3. *Horse-radish Butter*
Puree 4 ozs. horse-radish and blend into 1 lb. of butter.

4. *Shrimp Butter*
Puree 8 ozs. of cooked, shelled, and deveined shrimp and blend
with 8 ozs. of butter.

5. *Caviar Butter*
Blend 6 ozs. of caviar which has been pureed with 10 ozs. of
sweet butter.

6. *Curry Butter*
Sauté in clarified butter one finely chopped small onion until
lightly glazed. Add 2 tsp. of curry powder and simmer for a
minute or two, cool, puree this mixture and blend with 1 lb. of
butter.

7. *Pimento Butter*
Puree 8 ozs. of canned pimento peppers and blend with 8 ozs.
of butter.

8. *Paprika Butter*
Dissolve 1 tbs. of Spanish paprika in a little white wine to form
a paste and then blend into 1 lb. of butter.

9. *Garlic Butter*   4 oz
Puree approximately half a head of garlic and then blend it with
1 lb. of butter.

10. *Green Butter* (Montpelier)
Place in boiling water 1 oz. each of watercress, parsley, chervil,
chives, and tarragon, 1¼ oz. of chopped shallots and ¾ oz. of
fresh spinach leaves. Boil for 3 min., then drain *thoroughly*. Add
1 tbs. of capers, 3–4 ozs. of gherkins, a clove of garlic, and 5
anchovy filets, puree all ingredients. Add this to 1 lb. of butter.
Finally, fold in the pureed yolks of 5 hard boiled eggs and 8 ozs.
of olive oil. Season with salt, pepper, cayenne, and nutmeg.

11. *Nutmeg Butter*
    Grate finely two nutmegs and blend with 1 lb. of butter.

12. *Mustard Butter*
    Dissolve 2 tbs. of English mustard in a few drops of water and
    then blend into 1 lb. of butter.

13. *Truffle Butter* (Perigordine)
    Puree 8 small truffles and the yolks of 8 hard boiled eggs and
    then blend with 1 lb. of butter.

14. *Tarragon Butter*
    Blanche 10 ozs. of fresh tarragon, drain thoroughly and puree.
    Add 1 lb. of butter.

15. *Sardine Butter*
    Puree 30 sardine filets (boneless) and blend with 1 lb. of butter.

16. *Tuna Butter*
    Puree 8 ozs. of canned tuna (olive oil pack) and blend with 1 lb.
    of butter.

17. *Caviar Butter* (Muscovite)
    Puree 8 ozs. of caviar, 10 yolks of hard boiled eggs, and a pinch
    of cayenne pepper. Blend into 1 lb. of butter.

18. *Chive Butter*
    Finely chop one small bunch of chives and blend it with 1 lb.
    of butter.

19. *Onion Butter*
    Finely chop or puree one large Bermuda onion and blend it
    into 1 lb. of butter.

20. *Wine Butter*
    Slowly whip into 1 lb. of butter, according to taste and desired
    consistency, a fine red or white dry wine.

21. *Mint Butter*
Finely chop 8 tbs. of fresh mint and blend well with 1 lb. of butter.

22. *Lemon Butter*
Blend 8 tbs. of strained fresh lemon juice with 1 lb. of butter.

23. *Tomato Butter*
3 tbs. of tomato paste, 1 tbs. of lemon juice, blend with 1 lb. of butter.

24. *Roquefort Butter*
Mash 4 ozs. of Roquefort cheese and blend thoroughly with 1 lb. of butter.

25. *Shallot Butter*
Finely mince 2 ozs. shallots, ½ oz. garlic, and ½ oz. parsley. Blend thoroughly with 1 lb. of butter.

Cream may be used as a partial substitute for a portion of the butter in the following proportions: For every 2 ozs. (½ of a stick) of butter that is used, add 2 tbs. of heavy cream and in finishing fold in 3 tbs. of whipped cream. Naturally, a much richer product results. However, care must be taken in the storage of these "creams" as they have a tendency to spoil rather easily.

This brings up the point of advance preparation. To obtain the finest in flavor and quality, it is advisable to prepare the butters just before using, whenever possible. When absolutely necessary, these butters may be made up a day or two in advance and refrigerated at temperatures of about 38°F.

Butter itself can be frozen and thawed without too great a change in flavor or texture. However, when other ingredients have been mixed with the butter, the picture changes considerably since the mixtures tend to separate when thawed.

All the above recipes can be altered to suit by changing the ratios or by the addition of items such as lemon juice, Tabasco sauce, Worcestershire sauce, English mustard, horse-radish, and pepper.

3. Spreads

TO attempt to limit the quantity of possible spreads is an attempt to stifle the ingenuity and imagination of the culinary artist. To any basic spread, the individual needs only to add his own inspired touch. One should never have any fear of experimenting. He should try to combine unthought-of ingredients. A bland and a sharp taste complement each other with unexpected flavor.

When serving a variety of spreads in partitioned plates or small individual bowls, arrange the breads, crackers, and toast rounds in careful patterns on a bread board or wicker basket. Alternate rows of small squares of dark pumpernickel with melba toast rounds, and white finger toast with miniature rye slices. Be careful that breads are not allowed to dry out and curl at the edges. Butter a smaller supply and replenish often. The number of cocktail and canapé crackers put out by the national baking houses can add great variety to the party bread basket. Thus, interesting flavor combinations can be left to the guests' own ingenuity.

1. *Crab Meat Spread* (yield 1½ cups approx.)

    1 lb. backfin lump crab meat (broken up finely)
    3 tbs. finely chopped parsley
    2 tbs. finely chopped onion
    4 tbs. mayonnaise
    ½ tsp. lemon juice—pinch curry powder

In a bowl mix all ingredients together until well blended. Refrigerate until served.

2. *A-1 Spread*   (1½ cups approx.)

   12 ozs. cream cheese
   4 ozs. A-1 steak sauce

In a bowl blend together the ingredients until they are smooth.
Refrigerate until served.

3. *Cheddar Spread* (*May Be Frozen*)   (1½ cups approx.)

   8 ozs. sharp cheddar finely grated
   1 tsp. Worcestershire sauce
   1 tsp. finely chopped onion
   ½ tsp. Tabasco
   ½ tbs. tarragon vinegar

Mix all ingredients together in a bowl until everything is thoroughly blended. Refrigerate until served.

4. *Peanut Butter—Chili Spread*   (1 cup)

   ¾ cup chunk-style peanut butter
   ¼ cup chili sauce

Blend peanut butter and chili sauce until smooth. Refrigerate
until served.

5. *Shrimp Spread* (*May Be Frozen*)   (2 cups approx.)

   2 cups of cooked finely diced deveined shrimp
   ½ cup butter (softened)
   2 tbs. lemon juice
   1 tsp. salt
   ½ tsp. paprika (Spanish)
   2 tsp. Worcestershire
   2 tsp. mustard (prepared)

In a bowl blend all ingredients together until smooth. Refrigerate.

6. *Chile—Cottage Cheese Spread*   (2 cups approx.)

   2 cups cottage cheese
   3 tbs. chili sauce
   1 small onion finely diced

Whip all ingredients until completely smooth. (The use of an electric blender or mixer is advised.) Refrigerate.

7. *Ham—Peanut Butter Spread*   (2 cups approx.)

   5 ozs. deviled ham (commercial canned)
   6 ozs. peanut butter (chunk or smooth)
   4 ozs. mayonnaise
   5 tbs. finely diced dill pickle

Mix all ingredients together until thoroughly blended. Refrigerate.

8. *Anchovy Spread*   (1⅓ cups approx.)

   1 cup of soft butter
   4 tbs. pureed anchovies
   2 tbs. pureed onion
   ½ cup pureed celery

Puree anchovies, onion, and celery until smooth. Add to the butter and mix well. Refrigerate.

9. *Chicken—Bacon Spread*   (2 cups approx.)

   2 cups minced boiled chicken
   6 slices of crisp bacon crumbled fine
   ½ tsp. salt
   ½ cup mayonnaise
   ½ diced peeled apple

Combine all ingredients (except apple, which is added at time of service). Mix until smooth. Refrigerate.

10. *Egg Spread*   (2 cups approx.)

> 12 yolks hard boiled and strained
> 2 tsp. horse-radish
> 2 tsp. finely minced onion
> 2 tsp. Worcestershire sauce
> ½ cup mayonnaise
> 2 ozs. butter
> ½ tsp. salt

Combine all ingredients in bowl, mix until smooth. Refrigerate.

11. *Tuna Fish Spread*   (2 cups approx.)

> 2 cups tuna (canned Italian style in olive oil) drained
> 6 ozs. cream cheese
> 2 tbs. capers chopped
> 2 tbs. mayonnaise
> ½ tsp. Worcestershire sauce
> 2 tsp. horse-radish
> ½ small onion finely minced
> 2 cloves garlic pureed
> ½ tsp. celery salt

Blend all ingredients together until thoroughly mixed. Refrigerate until served.

12. *Salmon Spread*   (2¼ cups approx.)

> 2 cups flaked salmon
> 1 tbs. capers chopped
> 2 tbs. horse-radish
> 1 tbs. lemon juice
> 1 tbs. finely chopped parsley
> 2 ozs. (¼ cup) mayonnaise

Mix thoroughly until well blended. Refrigerate until served.

Salmon Spread

13. *Cottage Cheese Spread* (2 cups approx.)

2 cups cottage cheese
½ small onion finely chopped
1 tsp. parsley finely chopped
2 tbs. lemon juice
1 tsp. celery salt
¼ tsp. chives finely chopped
pinch pepper

Blend all ingredients thoroughly. Refrigerate until served.

14. *King Crab Spread* (*May Be Frozen*) (2½ cups approx.)

1 lb. king crab meat flaked
2½ tbs. mayonnaise
2½ tbs. horseradish
1 tsp. finely chopped parsley

1 tbs. lemon juice
½ tsp. celery salt
pinch pepper

Blend all ingredients together thoroughly. Refrigerate until served.

15. *Avocado Spread* (2¼ cups approx.)

2 large ripe avocados, peeled, pitted and mashed
2 small onions finely diced
1 clove garlic finely minced
2 tsp. lemon juice
1 tsp. salt
½ tbs. catsup
pinch pepper

Blend all ingredients together thoroughly. Refrigerate until served.

16. *Chicken Liver Spread* (*May Be Frozen*) (2 cups approx.)

12 fresh chicken livers chopped
3 tbs. butter
3 tbs. olive oil
¾ cup finely minced onion
1 tbs. dried leaf sage
⅔ cup white wine
1 tsp. finely chopped parsley

In butter and oil mixture, sauté the onions until lightly golden. Add livers and cook over high heat with caution. Add the sage, parsley, and wine; reduce heat until wine is evaporated over a moderate flame. Remove and cool. Should be served at room temperature or slightly warmed for full flavor. Adding 4 filets of anchovies to the onion and liver mix just before adding the wine gives a truly unique flavor.

17. *Pork Liver Spread* (*May Be Frozen*)   (2 cups approx.)

> 1 lb. finely chopped pork liver
> 1 clove garlic finely chopped
> 8 anchovy filets
> 4 pimentos chopped
> 2 tbs. olive oil
> ½ tsp. salt
> ¼ tsp. pepper
> 1 tsp. marjoram
> water

Sauté in olive oil the liver, garlic, anchovies, and pimentos for about 5 min. Add marjoram, salt, and pepper and continue cooking until browned. Add a little water as needed to insure a spreading consistency; simmer a few minutes longer and remove from heat. Serve slightly cooled or at room temperature—not chilled.

18. *Sicilian Caponatina Spread*   (2 cups)

> 4 small egg plants
> 1 cup olive oil
> 4 finely sliced onions
> ½ cup tomato sauce
> 4 stalks celery finely diced
> ½ cup capers
> 14 large green olives pitted and cut in pieces
> 2 tbs. pine nuts
> ½ cup wine vinegar
> ¼ cup sugar
> 1 tsp. salt
> ½ tsp. pepper

Peel and dice egg plant and fry in the hot olive oil. Remove the egg plant and add the onions and brown gently. Add the tomatoes and celery and cook until the celery is tender. Add a little water if necessary. Add capers, olives, nuts, and egg plant. Heat vinegar separately and dissolve sugar in it. Pour vinegar mix over egg plant. Add salt and pepper and simmer 20 min. Cool before serving.

19. *Sardine Spread*   (2 cups approx.)

> 1½ cups of canned sardines (mashed)
> ½ cup mayonnaise
> 2 tbs. lemon juice
> 1 tsp. finely chopped parsley

Mix all ingredients together in a bowl. Blend thoroughly. Refrigerate until served.

20. *Cucumber Spread*   (2 cups approx.)

> 2 cucumbers peeled and grated
> ¼ tsp. salt
> 1 cup cream cheese
> ½ cup finely chopped green pepper
> ¼ cup finely chopped onion
> pinch pepper, paprika, and Worcestershire sauce

Drain liquid from cucumbers and discard. Mix cucumber pulp and rest of ingredients thoroughly to insure it being well blended. Refrigerate until served.

Most spreads can be made up a few days in advance. However, as in the cases of the butters, it is advisable to prepare the spreads as close to using time as is possible. Again, freezing is not recommended because of the danger of separation.

4. Dips 𝒳

IT must be remembered in the preparation of dips that the consistency of the dip is all important. It cannot be too thick nor too thin. If a dip is too thick, the addition of a few drops of milk or consommé will act as a thinner and bring it to the proper consistency. On the other hand, if the dip is too thin, it can be tightened up by increasing the amount of the main thickening ingredient, which in most cases is the cream cheese.

Presentation of the dips is also of great importance. The dip should be garnished properly to produce color and eye appeal, surrounded by the various "dippers" to be used, and should be centered on the table to facilitate service for each guest.

The selection and preparation of the dippers can be a novel and enjoyable task as the combinations and varieties of the foods that can be used are practically endless. Several small trays with colorful assortments are more hospitable than one large out-sized arrangement. The essence of table hospitality is to see that each guest, the timid as well as the bold, has ready access to the food presented. All cocktail tidbits, particularly the do-it-yourself varieties, such as the dips and spreads, should never be placed more than an arm's length from the guest. An axiom for gracious hospitality at the cocktail hour might well be: "Table service *here*—family reach *at home*."

Suggested dippers follow (however, the list is as wide open as food and imagination combined can offer):

15

potato chips
corn chips
fried bacon rinds
French fried potato sticks

raw cauliflower buds
scallions
pickles (sticks, disks, or whole)
radishes
zucchini sticks or slices
cucumber slices or sticks
celery hearts
tomato wedges
turnip slices
carrot slices or sticks
endive leaves
romaine leaves
green pepper strips
watercress sprigs
cooked or canned asparagus tips
cooked or canned green beans

pretzels (stick or round)
melbas (round, long, square, etc.)
Saltine crackers
triscuits
sesame wafers
onion wafers
toast fingers
miniature rye slices
French bread rounds
garlic bread rounds

chicken chunks
tuna chunks
shrimps
turkey chunks
lobster chunks

avocado chunks (lemon dipped)
apple chunks (lemon dipped)
pear chunks
assorted melon chunks
pineapple chunks

1. *Cheese and Sardine Dip*   (2 cups approx.)

6½ ozs. sardines
6 ozs. cream cheese
3 tbs. onion finely minced
1 clove garlic finely minced
2 tbs. Worcestershire sauce
1 tbs. lemon juice
pinch salt and pepper

Split sardines lengthwise, remove center bone, and then mash sardines and blend thoroughly with all other ingredients. Refrigerate until served.

2. *Cold Clam Dip*   (2½ cups approx.)

12 ozs. cream cheese

¾ cup of steamed, drained, and minced chowder clams (or canned minced clams)
3 tsp. lemon juice
1 clove garlic finely minced
⅓ cup of clam broth
2 tsp. Worcestershire sauce
salt and pepper

Blend all ingredients together thoroughly. Refrigerate until served. If a thinner mix is desired, add more clam broth.

3. *Garlic Dip*   (2½ cups approx.)

6 cloves garlic pureed
12 ozs. cream cheese
1⅓ cups sour cream

Blend all ingredients together until thoroughly mixed. Refrigerate until served.

4. *Roquefort—Sour Cream Dip*   (2½ cups approx.)

5 ozs. Roquefort crumbled
1 lb. cottage cheese
½ cup sour cream
1 tbs. finely minced onion

Blend all ingredients together thoroughly. Refrigerate until ready for service.

5. *Avocado Dip*   (2½ cups approx.)

1 ripe medium-sized avocado
2 tbs. lemon juice
6 ozs. cream cheese
½ tsp. finely minced onion
salt and pepper
few drops of milk if needed as a thinner

Roquefort—Sour Cream Dip

Peel, pit, and mash the avocado, add lemon juice. Then blend all ingredients together and beat until smooth and creamy. Refrigerate until time to serve. (To improve color, a few drops of liquid green food color may be added if desired.)

6. ***Peanut Butter—Chili Sauce Dip***   (2½ cups)

    1¼ cups chunk or smooth peanut butter
    1¼ cups chili sauce

Blend together until smooth and refrigerate until served.

7. ***Tuna—Olive Dip***   (2½ cups approx.)

    1½ cups tuna (Italian style)
    ½ cup butter or mayonnaise
    ½ cup chopped pimento-stuffed olives

Blend all ingredients together thoroughly and refrigerate until needed.

8. *Chili—Horse-radish Dip*   (2½ cups approx.)

    1½ cups chili sauce
    ¾ cup horse-radish
    1 tbs. Worcestershire sauce
    1 tbs. finely minced onion
    1 clove garlic pureed
    1 tsp. salt
    3 tbs. distilled vinegar
    1 tsp. Tabasco
    2 tsp. celery salt
    6 tbs. very fine sugar

Blend all ingredients together until thoroughly mixed and refrigerate until served. (Note: If this dip is made up several days
in advance and kept refrigerated the flavor will improve.)

9. *Zesty Mayonnaise and Sour Cream Dip*   (2½ cups approx.)

    2 cloves garlic finely minced
    1 tsp. salt
    1 cup sour cream
    1½ cups mayonnaise
    ⅔ cup finely chopped parsley
    6 tbs. finely chopped chives
    6 tbs. finely chopped tarragon leaves
    8 anchovies pureed
    2 tsp. Worcestershire
    1 tsp. dry mustard

Blend all ingredients together thoroughly and refrigerate until
service time.

10. *Sharp Mayonnaise Dip*   (2½ cups)

    2 cups mayonnaise
    ¼ cup distilled vinegar
    5 tsp. prepared mustard
    2 tbs. dill
    salt and pepper

Blend all ingredients together till well blended and smooth. Refrigerate until served.

11. *Chicken Liver Dip*   (2½ cups)

> 1½ cups finely chopped cooked chicken livers
> 3 tsp. finely minced onion
> 4 tsp. finely minced dill pickle
> 2 tbs. pickle juice
> ¾ cup mayonnaise
> dash Tabasco
> 3 hard boiled eggs finely chopped
> salt and pepper

Blend all ingredients thoroughly and refrigerate until served.

12. *Simple Cream Cheese Dip*   (2½ cups)

> 12 ozs. cream cheese
> 6 tbs. heavy cream
> 3 tbs. mayonnaise
> 1 tsp. Spanish paprika
> 2 cloves of garlic pureed
> 2 tsp. Worcestershire sauce
> 2 tbs. prepared mustard
> 1 tbs. lemon juice

Cream the cheese and heavy cream till smooth. Blend in all other ingredients and refrigerate until served.

13. *Cream Cheese—Chive and Egg Dip*   (2½ cups)

> 12 ozs. cream cheese
> 4 hard boiled eggs finely chopped
> 3 tbs. finely chopped chives
> 2 tsp. prepared mustard
> 1 tsp. Worcestershire
> salt and pepper
> (a few drops of milk may be added as a thinner)

Cream the cream cheese and blend in other ingredients till smooth and even. Refrigerate until served.

14. *Barbecue Dip*   (2½ cups approx.)

> ⅔ cup vinegar (cider)
> ¾ cup water
> 3 tbs. very fine sugar
> 2 tbs. prepared mustard
> ¾ tsp. black pepper
> 2½ tsp. salt
> ½ tsp. cayenne pepper
> 2 onions finely sliced
> ¼ cup butter
> ¾ cup catsup
> 4 tbs. Worcestershire
> 1 lemon sliced in "wheels"

Simmer in a saucepan the vinegar, water, sugar, mustard, pepper, salt, cayenne, lemon, onion, and butter. Allow to simmer for 30 min. Uncover, add catsup and Worcestershire and bring to a boil. Remove from heat and cool.

15. *Shrimp and Cheese Dip*   (2½ cups approx.)

> ¾ lb. cooked shrimp (peeled and deveined)
> 1½ cups cottage cheese
> 5 tbs. chili sauce
> ¾ tsp. minced onion
> ¾ tsp. lemon juice
> ½ tsp. Worcestershire sauce
> salt, pepper, and milk

Finely chop the shrimp and mix all ingredients together until smooth and thoroughly blended. Add a few drops of milk, if necessary, to insure proper consistency. Refrigerate until served.

Blue Cheese Dip (at top) and assorted dips

16. *Roquefort—Cottage Cheese—Sour Cream Dip*   (2½ cups)

   5 ozs. Roquefort or Blue cheese
   2 cups cottage cheese
   1 tsp. finely minced onion
   ½ cup sour cream

Crumble Roquefort and blend with other ingredients until smooth and well blended. Refrigerate until served.

17. *A Smooth Cheese Dip*   (2½ cups approx.)

   8 ozs. cream cheese
   2 cups sour cream
   1 clove garlic pureed
   salt and pepper
   dash Tabasco
   dash Worcestershire

In a blender, or with a wire whip, blend all ingredients together until smooth. Refrigerate until served.

18. *Blue Cheese—Mayonnaise Dip*   (2½ cups approx.)

    ¼ lb. Blue cheese
    5 tbs. heavy cream
    ¾ cup mayonnaise
    2 tsp. prepared mustard
    ¼ tsp. salt
    ¼ tsp. pepper
    ¼ cup wine vinegar
    ¼ cup vegetable oil

Blend all ingredients together until smooth and creamy. Refrigerate until served.

19. *Sour Cream and Onion Dip*   (2½ cups approx.)

    2 cups sour cream
    1 cup onion finely minced
    3 tbs. distilled vinegar
    1 tsp. celery salt
    salt and pepper

Blend all ingredients until smooth. Refrigerate until served.

20. *Mint and Sour Cream Dip*   (2½ cups approx.)

    2½ cups sour cream
    4 tbs. finely chopped mint leaves
    1½ tsp. sugar
    1½ tsp. lemon juice
    1 tsp. salt

Blend all ingredients together. Refrigerate until served.

21. *Cheddar Cheese and Mayonnaise Dip*   (2½ cups approx.)

    2 cups mayonnaise
    6 ozs. Cheddar cheese grated

4 tbs. vinegar (distilled)
1 clove of garlic pureed
½ tsp. salt
1 tsp. Worcestershire

Blend all ingredients together until thoroughly incorporated.
Refrigerate until served.

22. *Whipped Cream and Olive Dip*   (2½ cups approx.)

1⅓ cups of chopped pitted ripe olives
1 cup heavy cream
2 tbs. lemon juice
2 tbs. sugar
6 tbs. mayonnaise
1 tbs. prepared mustard
dash Tabasco

Whip cream until thick but not too stiff; beat into cream all
other ingredients except olives until well incorporated. Finally,
fold in olives. Refrigerate until served.

23. *Cheddar and Walnut Dip*   (2½ cups approx.)

2 cups Cheddar cheese (grated)
6 ozs. cream cheese
¼ cup sour cream
1 clove garlic pureed
½ tsp. Spanish paprika
1 tsp. Worcestershire
1 cup walnuts finely chopped

Combine all ingredients and mix well. Refrigerate until served.

24. *Pineapple—Tuna Fish Dip*   (2½ cups approx.)

9 ozs. drained crushed canned pineapple
3 tbs. pineapple juice
4 ozs. cream cheese
4 ozs. cottage cheese

1 can tuna
½ cup avocado diced
salt, pepper, and nutmeg

Blend all ingredients together until smooth. Refrigerate until served.

25. *Cream Cheese and Watercress*   (2½ cups)

6 ozs. cream cheese
4 tbs. milk
½ lb. bacon slices crumbled
½ cup chopped watercress
½ tsp. grated onion

Combine all ingredients together blending well. Refrigerate until served.

5. From the Chafing Dish

THE ideal service for the cocktail hour would include individual chafing dishes graded as to size for couples, foursomes, or larger. This would personalize the service, giving each guest the glow that comes from individual attention.

Where this service is not possible, waiters may serve directly from a tray or chafing dishes holding assorted delights. This will require the vigilant attention of each waiter to his station so that he may foresee his guests' wishes.

The remaining presentation is of course a central table, effectively decorated with large chafing dishes, attended by a chef or trained waiter so that each guest may arrange a form of "do-it-yourself" service in his selection.

1. *Shrimp Stuffed Grey Sole Rolls*   (20 portions)

> 2 lbs. 8 ozs. cooked shrimp chopped
> ¾ cup mayonnaise
> 20 filets of grey sole
> 1 cup white wine
> Tabasco, clarified butter melted
> Accent, paprika (Spanish)
> salt and white pepper

(1) Combine shrimps and mayonnaise and blend thoroughly.
(2) Spread the mixture down the center of each filet, and then sprinkle a few drops of Tabasco over each, to taste.

(3) Roll up and place seam side down in a shallow baking pan. Pour the wine over the filets and then brush each with the melted clarified butter. Add salt, pepper, Accent, and paprika and place in the oven at 400° for approximately 20 min., or until the fish can be easily flaked with a fork. Remove to the chafing dish; gently place each filet in the chafing dish, seam side down, and pour juices over the filets. If more liquid is needed, add a little white wine. Arrange a few sprigs of parsley over the fish, cover, and keep hot in the chafing dish until serving time. (One filet per person.)

This dish can be cooked directly in the chafing dish if desired. However, when dealing with large quantities, it is advisable to cook as directed and then transfer to the chafing dish.

2. *Chicken À La King*   (20 portions)

> 1 lb. sliced mushrooms (canned or fresh; drained wt. if canned)
> 1 lb. melted clarified butter
> 12 ozs. flour
> 1 qt. chicken stock (hot)
> 2 qts. milk (hot)
> 1 pt. light cream (hot)
> ½ lb. green peppers thinly sliced
> 4 ozs. Spanish pimentos thinly sliced
> 4 ozs. sherry wine
> 4 lbs. cooked boneless chicken meat sliced
> salt and pepper to taste
> dash Worcestershire and Tabasco

(1) Sauté mushrooms in the melted clarified butter with a few drops of lemon juice until soft and tender.
(2) Add flour to make a roux, stir well and simmer gently for about 10 min., taking care it does not brown.
(3) Slowly pour in the hot stock, stirring until mixture is smooth and slightly thickened.

(4) Stir in milk and cream and blend well.
(5) Cook green peppers in boiling water for about 5 min. or until tender. Drain.
(6) Add peppers and pimentos and sherry to the sauce and season to taste.
(7) Add chicken meat to the sauce, folding it in carefully to prevent breaking it up.
(8) Keep hot in chafing dish.

3. *Cubed Lamb Viennese Style*   (20 portions)

6 lbs. lamb shoulder cut in 1 in. cubes
6 tbs. lard
6 tbs. clarified butter
3 cups of finely chopped onions
1 tbs. Hungarian paprika
salt, pepper, Worcestershire to taste

(1) Coat lamb in flour, and sauté in the hot lard until well browned.
(2) Add the onions, paprika, salt, pepper, and Worcestershire. Barely cover with hot water and simmer slowly until tender.

4. *Fried Mozzarella*   (20 portions)

3 lbs. Mozzarella (loaf shape preferred)
2 cups flour
8 eggs (beaten)
1 tsp. salt
4 cups breadcrumbs
3 cups olive oil

(1) Slice Mozzarella about 2 in. thick.
(2) Coat each slice generously with flour, dip in eggs, and then in breadcrumbs. Repeat the process and then fry in the olive oil just long enough to obtain a deep golden color.

5. *Oriental Crab Meat Balls* (20 portions—¾ oz. balls)

    8 ozs. ground pork
    4 ozs. backfin crab meat
    ¼ cup finely chopped canned mushrooms
    ¼ cup finely chopped water chestnuts
    1 tsp. salt
    ½ tsp. sugar
    ½ tsp. pepper
    ¼ tsp. Accent
    ½ cup cornstarch or arrowroot
    1 egg beaten
    1 tbs. water

(1) Add water to the egg and reserve.
(2) Thoroughly blend the pork, crab meat, mushrooms, chestnuts, salt, sugar, pepper, and Accent until smooth.
(3) Form into small balls, about ¾ oz. each.
(4) Roll the balls in the cornstarch and then in the egg and water mixture.
(5) Deep fry at 350° until golden brown.
(6) Keep in warm chafing dish until served. Then spear each ball with a toothpick.

6. *Veal Scallopine Marsala* (20 portions)

    9 lbs. leg of veal cut into cutlets ⅛ in. thick
    olive oil (as needed)
    flour (as needed)
    6 large onions finely diced
    1 cup Marsala wine
    3 cloves garlic
    ¼ cup parsley finely chopped
    3 lbs. mushrooms peeled and thinly sliced

(1) Cut veal into 2 in. squares and dust liberally with flour.
(2) Heat the olive oil in a heavy pan and sauté the veal slices until they are deep rich brown. Add additional oil as is needed.

(3) Remove meat from pan and reserve.
(4) Sauté the onions in the same pan until lightly browned, adding more oil if necessary.
(5) Add mushrooms and mix well with the onions.
(6) Add the meat, garlic and marsala wine, salt, and pepper.
(7) Simmer gently, stirring until sauce thickens.
(8) Sprinkle with parsley and serve.

7. *Filet of Beef Stroganoff*   (20 portions)

> 5 lbs. filet of beef, cut into ¼ in. medallions
> 5 large onions sliced in julienne
> 1 cup olive oil
> 3 lbs. mushrooms finely sliced
> ½ cup flour
> 3 cups sour cream
> salt, pepper, Worcestershire, Accent to taste
> (2 tbs. meat glaze—optional)

(1) Sauté the julienne of onions in the olive oil, until well browned. Remove the onions and discard.
(2) In the same hot oil, sauté the filet of beef (which has been thoroughly coated with flour) until lightly browned. Add the sliced mushrooms and continue to sauté a few minutes longer.
(3) Season to taste. Lower the heat. Add the sour cream and meat glaze and cook for about 10 min. longer.

8. *Rice Pilaf*   (20 portions)

> 4 tbs. butter
> 2 large onions, finely diced
> 4 cups raw regular white rice
> 8 cups chicken consommé
> 2 bay leaves

(1) Sauté the onion in the butter until lightly glazed.
(2) Add the rice and mix well.
(3) Add the consommé and bring to a boil—stirring well.
(4) Remove from heat. Add the bay leaves and *cover pot.*

(5) Bake at 400° for 25 min.

(6) Remove from oven. Fluff up and place in chafing dish.

(Note: This is a base or side dish for most hot chafing dishes.)

9. *Stuffed Cabbage* (20 portions)

> 20 large outside cabbage leaves
> 2½ lbs. ground beef
> 3 tbs. cooked white rice
> 5 tbs. sugar
> 5 tbs. finely diced onion
> 3 tbs. lemon juice
> 1 tsp. Spanish paprika
> salt, pepper, Accent, and Worcestershire

(1) Steam cabbage leaves in hot water to make soft and pliable.

(2) Mix all the other ingredients together, blending thoroughly, and place scoopful of mixture on each cabbage leaf. Roll up each leaf and fold ends under, forming a neat bundle. Bake at 325° in oven for 2 hrs. with a savory tomato sauce. [See tomato sauce for stuffed cabbage.]

10. *Tomato Sauce for Stuffed Cabbage* (20 portions)

> 2 ozs. bacon fat (rendered)
> 2 large onions finely diced
> 1½ tsp. salt
> 1 tsp. paprika
> ½ tsp. pepper
> 1 cup water
> 4 cans (8 ozs. each) of Spanish style tomato sauce (Hunts, Del Monté, etc.
> ½ cup granulated sugar
> ½ cup lemon juice

(1) In bacon fat, sauté the onions until tender. Add spices and water.

(2) Then add tomatoes, lemon juice, and sugar. Mix well.

(3) Place cabbage leaves seam side down in the oven pan and spoon over the tomato sauce.

(4) Bake for 2 hrs.

(5) Remove to a chafing dish and serve warm.

11. *Manicotti* [see Cheese Filling, below]   (18 to 20 portions)

Crepes

>   2 eggs
>   1 tbs. melted clarified butter
>   ⅔ cup milk
>   ½ cup flour
>   ¼ tsp. salt

(1) Whip eggs thoroughly and then add milk and shortening. Sift the flour and salt into the egg mixture. Beat until smooth.

(2) Heat up small 5 in. egg pans, lightly greased, and drop in crepe batter by the spoonful—just enough to barely coat the bottom of the pan. Cook, turning it once, until a very light golden tan color. Remove and lay flat on the work table and add the cheese filling [see Cheese Filling, below] with the aid of a pastry bag and plain tube. Then roll the crepe up and place in a chafing dish, seam side down. Add some savory tomato sauce [see Tomato Sauce, below] and heat up thoroughly, about 20 min. Serve with sauce and sprinkle with Parmesan cheese.

Cheese Filling

>   1 lb. ricotta cheese
>   ½ lb. Mozzarella cheese finely chopped
>   4 tbs. Parmesan cheese
>   1 tbs. finely chopped parsley
>   2 egg yolks
>   salt and pepper to taste

Mix all ingredients together until smooth and well blended. Keep refrigerated until ready to use.

Tomato Sauce

>   1½ lbs. equal portions of beef and pork chopped
>   1½ tbs. olive oil

2 cloves garlic
1 med. onion finely chopped
1 tsp. finely chopped parsley
1 lg. can Italian tomatoes
¾ tsp. chopped basil
salt and pepper to taste
½ tsp. fennel seed
1 tbs. butter

(1) Place tomatoes in a pot and cook slowly over moderate heat until they "tighten up" (water evaporates) and the tomatoes reach the proper consistency.

(2) In a heavy bottomed pan, sauté the chopped meat until lightly browned. Remove and sauté the onions and garlic until browned. Add more oil if needed. Place meat back in pan and mix well with the onion and garlic. Add the parsley and remove from heat.

(3) Puree the tomatoes by forcing through a fine china cap or colander. Add the pureed tomatoes to the beef and pork mixture and mix well. Place back on fire and cook slowly for 1 hr. after adding fennel and basil leaves. Add butter just before using.

12. *Eggrolls*   (15 portions)

Skins

1 lb. flour (all-purpose)
2 eggs well beaten
1 tsp. salt
8 ozs. (1 cup) ice water

(1) Sift flour and salt together. Add eggs to this and blend well.
(2) Add the ice water and mix the dough until it is quite firm and very smooth.
(3) Roll the dough out until it is paper thin. Make sure the dough is well floured as you work it.
(4) Cut into 6 in. squares and stock them in the refrigerator, well floured and wrapped in wax paper, until ready to fill.

(5) Place about 1 oz. (4 tbs.) of the filling in the center of each 6 in. square skin and fold over the filling with the skin edge nearest you. Brush the edges with beaten egg and then fold both sides toward the center. Then roll close and tight. The roll should not be more than 2 in. in diameter.

(6) Deep fat fry at 350° until lightly browned. (Turning if it is necessary.) Drain well and remove to chafing dish to keep warm until served.

Filling

    1½ lbs. finely chopped cooked shrimp or crab meat
    3 tbs. finely chopped scallions or onion
    3 tbs. cornstarch
    2 eggs well beaten
    salt and pepper to taste
    a few drops soy sauce

(1) Dissolve cornstarch in the eggs.
(2) Add all the ingredients together mixing well.

13. *Southern Crab Cakes* (20 portions)

    5 cups backfin crab meat
    1 tbs. salt
    1 tbs. dry mustard
    1 tbs. Worcestershire sauce
    3 egg yolks
    3 tbs. mayonnaise
    1½ tbs. finely chopped parsley
    flour
    breadcrumbs } as much as is needed
    beaten eggs

(1) Mix all ingredients together thoroughly and form into 20 firm cakes. Chill well.
(2) Dust cakes with flour. Then dip in beaten eggs and finally in breadcrumbs.

(3) Sauté cakes in a pan with a little melted clarified butter over high heat until golden brown. Turn once. Remove to chafing dish to keep hot until served.

14. *Shrimp and Proscuitto*   (20 portions)

    20 extra large shrimps peeled and veined (under 10 to the lb.)
    20 thin slices of proscuitto
    ¾ cup brandy
    20 fresh leaves of basil
    salt, pepper, lemon juice, and breadcrumbs
    20 small sprigs of parsley

(1) Carefully wash the shrimps and then allow them to marinate in the brandy for about 2 hrs.
(2) Remove the shrimps and wrap each one in a slice of proscuitto.
(3) Lay a basil leaf on each and sprinkle lightly with breadcrumbs seasoned with salt and pepper.
(4) Bake in a very hot oven (500°) for about 10 min., or until breadcrumbs brown.
(5) Remove from the oven, sprinkle with lemon juice, and garnish with fresh parsley sprigs. Serve hot.

15. *Lamb Curry*   (20 portions)

    6 tbs. melted shortening
    6 lbs. lamb breast cut in cubes
    6 qts. water
    1 tbs. salt
    1½ tsp. pepper
    2 tbs. crushed mint leaves
    1 tbs. ginger (powdered)
    1 lb. finely chopped onions
    2 cups flour
    1 tbs. curry powder
    ¾ cup water

(1) Brown the meat in the shortening in a heavy bottomed pan.
(2) Barely cover the meat with water and add the onions, salt, pepper, ginger, and mint and allow to simmer for about 1½ hrs.

(3) Strain off the broth and reserve 4 cups.

(4) Mix the curry and flour together and dissolve the mixture with the remaining ¾ cup of water. Stir until it is smooth. Stir in the 4 cups of the lamb broth and again mix well until smoothly blended. Add this to the lamb in a chafing dish and cook until thickened and well heated.

16. *Codfish Balls*   (about 50 1½ in. balls)

>   2 cups shredded codfish
>   4 cups diced raw potatoes
>   2 eggs plus 1 yolk beaten
>   3 tbs. clarified butter
>   1 clove garlic pureed
>   ¼ tsp. English mustard (dry)
>   1 tsp. ground dill seed
>   ¼ tsp. celery salt
>   salt and pepper to taste
>   pinch cayenne and nutmeg
>   flour, 1 beaten egg, 2 tbs. water, and pinch of salt
>   1 cup breadcrumbs

(1) Cook potatoes until tender

(2) Cook cod in about 1 in. of water for 10 min.

(3) Rice the potatoes and add the cod

(4) Whip well, then add the eggs, butter, and seasonings, blending until smooth.

(5) Chill mixture for about 2 hrs., until firm.

(6) Roll into 1½ in. balls, and roll them in flour, egg, and water mixture and finally into the breadcrumbs.

(7) Deep fry at 350° until golden brown.

(8) Drain, remove to a chafing dish to keep hot until served. Serve skewered on a toothpick.

17. *Hot Proscuitto Hors D'Oeuvres*

Have proscuitto sliced paper thin. Slice each piece in half to resemble a strip of bacon. Then, using toothpicks, secure the proscuitto slices around any of these items of food: sliced pear chunks, pineapple chunks, cooked shrimp, canned mushroom caps, peach chunks, cooked chicken livers, melon chunks, canned luncheon meat chunks, pearl onions, raw oysters, or almost anything else you can think of. When ready, broil these proscuitto wrapped tidbits until the fat on the proscuitto is melted and they are well heated. Remove to a chafing dish and serve hot.

18. *Cocktail Meat Balls* (25 1½ in. balls)

    1 lb. ground chuck
    ½ tsp. Tabasco sauce
    2 tbs. finely chopped onion
    1 tbs. chili sauce
    1 tsp. salt
    ¼ tsp. black pepper
    1 tbs. finely chopped parsley
    1 tbs. olive oil
    2 tbs. flour
    1 cup water
    ½ tsp. Tabasco
    ¼ tsp. salt
    2 tbs. mustard (prepared with horse-radish)
    ½ tsp. Worcestershire
    ¼ tsp. celery salt

(1) Mix thoroughly the chuck, ½ tsp. Tabasco, onion, chili, 1 tsp. salt, black pepper and parsley. Then shape this mix into 1½ in. balls. Chill for 1 hr.

(2) Brown the meat balls in the hot olive oil a few at a time. Remove when done.

(3) In the drippings and olive oil, add the flour and stir well. Then add water and cook until this mixture thickens. Add all the rest of the ingredients. Mix well and place the meat balls in this mixture. Simmer 10 min. and serve on buttered noodles.

19. *Crab Meat Dewey*   (20 portions)

     3 lbs. lump crab meat
     1½ cups finely sliced green pepper
     6 ozs. sherry wine
     1½ cups finely sliced pimentos
     1½ lbs. finely sliced mushrooms
     5 egg yolks
     6 ozs. butter
     3 cups med. cream sauce
     salt and pepper to taste
     1 tbs. lemon juice
     pinch of nutmeg

(1) Sauté mushrooms in butter with the lemon juice for a few minutes.
(2) Add the green pepper and cook for several minutes until tender.
(3) Add crab meat, salt, pepper, and nutmeg.
(4) Jump ingredients in pan gently—stir with a spoon as little as possible.
(5) Add the cream sauce.
(6) Combine egg yolks with the sherry wine and add. Jump a few minutes longer to mix well.
(7) Decorate with the pimento slices and serve hot.

20. *Deviled Crab*   (20 portions)

     6 ozs. clarified butter
     3 lbs. lump crab meat
     2 cups light cream
     1½ tsp. paprika
     6 beaten eggs
     4½ tsp. prepared mustard
     3 ozs. flour
     ¼ tsp. English mustard
     ¼ tsp. cayenne pepper
     few drops Tabasco
     salt and pepper to taste

(1) Melt 3 ozs. butter in a pan and add the flour to form a roux.
(2) Slowly add the cream, stirring well to blend it with the flour. Simmer until the mixture is thick.
(3) Remove it from heat. Add the eggs, salt, pepper and cayenne, and paprika and mustard. Combine everything well.
(4) Add crab meat, blend, then place in a baking dish. Add the rest of the clarified butter and brown under the broiler. Serve hot.

21. *Mixed Seafood Newburg* (20 portions)

1 lb. lobster meat
1 lb. shrimps (raw, shelled, and veined)
½ lb. scallops
½ lb. filet sole
1 cup heavy cream
3 cups cream sauce
1 cup melted clarified butter
1 tbs. paprika
1 cup sherry wine
6 egg yolks
salt and pepper to taste

(1) Sauté all the seafood in the clarified butter until almost cooked.
(2) Add ½ cup sherry and simmer it until wine reduces by three-fourths.
(3) Add paprika and the cream sauce. Combine well and simmer for a few minutes.
(4) Combine yolks and heavy cream and add slowly to the first mixture, blending well. Add the rest of the sherry, check seasoning, and serve hot.

22. *Curried Shrimp* (20 portions)

3 lbs. cooked, shelled, and veined shrimp
1 lg. onion diced very fine
3 tbs. shredded coconut
3 apples finely diced (skin on)
3 tbs. melted clarified butter
1½ tsp. curry powder

3 cups cream sauce
salt and pepper to taste

(1) Sauté in the melted clarified butter the shrimp, apples, and onions until onions are glazed.
(2) Add the curry powder and coconut and mix well.
(3) Add the cream sauce. Combine thoroughly, season to taste, and serve hot.

23. *Clams Casino À La Felice* (20 portions)

Casino Butter

½ lb. softened butter
1 tbs. finely chopped shallots
½ tsp. finely chopped parsley
1 tbs. chopped pimento
1 tbs. finely chopped green pepper
½ clove garlic pureed
salt and pepper to taste and a few drops of lemon juice
6 slices bacon (raw) cut in 1 in. squares
40 clams on the half-shell

(1) Combine all ingredients except the bacon and the clams. Mix well and make sure everything is thoroughly incorporated.
(2) Place the entire mass on a piece of waxed paper and shape it into a long cylinder 1 in. in diameter.
(3) Place it in the refrigerator until firm.
(4) Have the open clams placed on a shallow pan and place a thin slice of the hardened casino butter over each clam. Top with a square of bacon and broil until the bacon is crisp. Serve hot.

24. *Baked Clams Oreganate* (20 portions)

40 clams on the half-shell
¾ cup breadcrumbs
2 tsp. salt
½ tsp. pepper
1½ tsp. Spanish paprika
2 tbs. finely chopped parsley

2 tsp. ground oregano
¾ tsp. pureed garlic
olive oil (enough to provide a proper consistency—mixture
    must be fluid enough to resemble a thick syrup)

(1) Mix all ingredients except the clams and the olive oil together.
    Blend them well.
(2) Add the olive oil, to produce the proper consistency, mixing
    well.
(3) On each clam, place about 1 tsp. of mix. Put in a shallow pan
    and bake at 450° for 8 to 10 min., or until the bread browns.

25. *Baked Spareribs with Barbecue Sauce*   (20 portions)

Cut up about 15 lbs. of spareribs. Place them in a roasting pan
with the meat side up. Thinly slice 5 lemons and 5 onions and
place them over the ribs. Roast in a very hot oven (500°) for
about 20 min. Pour off the excess fat at this point, and add about
1 qt. of barbecue sauce and continue baking at 375° for about
45 min., or until brown, basting often. Remove to chafing dish
and serve hot.

26. *Barbecue Sauce*   (1 qt.)

    1½ cups water
    ½ cup cider vinegar
    4 tbs. brown sugar
    2 tbs. prepared mustard
    1 tsp. pepper
    1 tbs. salt
    ½ tsp. cayenne pepper
    2 slices of lemon
    2 med. onions sliced
    ½ cup butter
    1 cup catsup
    6 tbs. Worcestershire sauce

(1) Mix all ingredients, except catsup and Worcestershire, and sim-
    mer uncovered for 20 min.
(2) Add Worcestershire and catsup and bring to a boil.

27. *Fondue*

> 2 cups of shredded Swiss or Gruyère cheese
> 4 tsp. of flour
> 1 clove of garlic
> 1 cup of dry white wine
> ¼ cup of kirsch
> salt
> freshly ground pepper

(1) Use a heavy earthenware pan that can be kept hot over an alcohol flame or use a chafing dish.
(2) Rub the pan well with the garlic.
(3) Pour in the wine and heat almost to a boil.
(4) Dredge the cheese with the flour and add slowly to the hot wine, stirring until the cheese is melted and thoroughly blended with the wine.
(5) Stir in the kirsch and continue heating until the mixture is thick and creamy.
(6) Season with the salt and pepper.
(7) Keep the mixture hot; if it becomes too thick, add more kirsch.
(8) Serve your guests chunks of French bread which they can spear with a fork and dunk in the fondue.

28. *Empanadas*

> 3 tbs. butter
> ½ cup onion minced
> 1 cup cooked beef or chicken
> ½ cup chopped stuffed olives
> ½ tsp. chili powder
> 1 tsp. Worcestershire sauce
> 2 hard cooked eggs
> 1 lb. pastry or pie dough

(1) Melt butter in pan, add onion, sauté lightly.
(2) Add all other ingredients except pastry; mix well.
(3) Cut 4 in. circles, brush edges with egg.
(4) Place 1 tbs. of mix in center.

(5) Fold over and seal edges well, crimping tightly.

(6) Fry in deep fat at 375° until browned and done.

(7) Drain on paper and keep warm.

29. *Caviar Crepes*

> 1 cup sifted flour
> ½ tsp. salt
> 4 eggs
> 2 cups of milk
> 2 tbs. melted butter
> caviar
> sour cream

(1) Sift flour and salt into a bowl.

(2) Beat the eggs and mix them into the flour with a whisk.

(3) Add milk, slowly beating it in and add butter. *It is best to let the batter stand for an hour or two before using.*

(4) Heat a small pan. Add a little butter and let it heat until it sizzles.

(5) Drop in about 2 tbs. of the batter, tilting the pan so that the batter spreads evenly and thinly.

(6) Bake quickly on both sides and keep the crepes warm in a very low oven until all are completed.

(7) Fill each crepe with a little caviar and roll up.

(8) Serve with a bowl of sour cream. The sour cream may be flavored with Tabasco if desired.

6. Canapés

THE canapé, which is the base of the Russian hors d'oeuvre, will offer the opportunity to use the butters and spreads which were presented in earlier chapters.

The canapé is usually made with a cracker-type biscuit or thin slices of bread toasted or untoasted. They can be offered in various shapes and forms and are buttered with the different types of butters and spreads made for hors d'oeuvres. The garnishings are limitless.

Today there is, ready to serve, a tremendous variety of crackers and breads. By employing these different bases, infinite variety can be added for both taste and eye appeal.

The pastry bag and fine star tube are, with the spatula and knife, indispensable tools used for the make-up of the canapé. They give the means for making the decoration professional and varied.

Varied spreads, as well as varied butters, may be used with almost any bread or cracker base of any shape or size by adding a topping of color and taste such as an olive slice or pickle slice or chopped parsley, etc. Literally hundreds of variations can be made. Imagination is the key word. To list all the varieties that could be made would be impossible, but by using the already mentioned canapés as sample patterns, an inviting display may be offered.

1. *Ribbon Canapé*

As in the checkerboard (see canapé no. 23), alternate 4 slices of bread, half white and half wheat. Smear with a spread or butter and trim off the edges. Cover with waxed paper and refrigerate until well chilled. Cut in ½ in. slices and serve.

Pinwheel Canapés (border) and assorted canapés

2. *Pinwheel Canapé*
Trim crusts from a pullman loaf and slice lengthwise about ⅛ in. thick. Press each slice with a rolling pin. Smear with a spread or butter and stuff if desired. Roll it up in jelly-roll fashion and wrap it up in waxed paper. Refrigerate until firm. When ready, cut into ½ in. slices and serve.

3. *Mosaic Canapé*
Using fancy cookie cutters, cut shapes from both white and wheat breads and remove centers of each if desired. Place contrasting pieces of bread, with spread or butter in between and then fill center with contrasting insert. Chill and serve.

4. *Anchovy Canapé*
Lightly butter a canapé with anchovy butter. Lay strips of anchovies on top and in the center place a sprinkling of finely

Mosaic Canapés

Anchovy Canapés (diamond, finger, star, and round)

sieved yolks of hard boiled eggs and an equal portion of finely chopped parsley (mimosa). Decorate the edges with anchovy butter piped out of the pastry bag.

5. **Shrimp Canapé**
   Butter a canapé lightly with shrimp butter. In the center, place some finely chopped cooked shrimp that has been blended with parsley and lemon juice. Border with piped out shrimp butter. (See also canapé No. 17.)

6. **Caviar Canapé**
   Butter a canapé lightly with caviar butter. Cover with a layer of caviar. Border with a mixture of chopped egg whites and yolks. Top with a sprinkle of chives.

7. **Caviar Cigarettes**
   On paper-thin slices of white bread, spread a light layer of caviar and then roll up tightly to resemble a cigarette.

8. **Canapé Rigoletto**
   Butter a canapé lightly with cayenne butter. Sprinkle with a mixture made up of finely chopped ham, tongue, egg whites, yolks, and truffle. Border with mimosa.

9. **Canapé À La Danoise**
   Butter a canapé made from a slice of cocktail rye with horse-radish butter. Arrange decoratively slices of smoked salmon, caviar, and filets of marinated herrings.

10. **Canapé of Crayfish**
    Butter a canapé with crayfish butter. Arrange slices of cooked crayfish tails on top and border with piped out crayfish butter.

11. **Canapé of Tongue**
    Butter a canapé with mustard butter. Arrange slices of tongue on top and decorate with mustard butter. (Note: By taking an

unsliced pullman loaf of bread and slicing it horizontally a large base for the making of quantities of canapés is provided. This base can then be cut with fancy cutters as desired.)

12. *Canapé of Ham*
Same as the tongue, but using ham instead.

13. *Canapé of Lobster*
Lightly butter a canapé with lobster butter. Arrange slices of cooked lobster meat on top. Border with mimosa.

14. *Canapé of Eggs*
Butter a canapé lightly with mayonnaise. Sprinkle the top with chopped egg whites and border with chopped yolks.

15. *Canapé of Eggs À La Gregoire*
Lightly butter a canapé with mustard butter. Place a slice of hard boiled egg on top. Garnish this with a swirl of mayonnaise. Border with mimosa.

16. *Anchovy and Pimento*
Spread a slice of toast with anchovy butter. Alternate anchovy filets and strips of pimento. Cut diagonally into fingers.

17. *Shrimp No. 2*
Spread an oblong cracker with pimento butter. Overlap a row of tiny cooked shrimp. Decorate the corners with small diamonds of pimento.

18. *Herring*
Spread small round slices of pumpernickel with onion butter. Top with a slice of pickled herring filet. Decorate with small strips of ripe olive.

19. *Tongue*
Spread rye bread circles with mustard butter. Place a slice of

Checkerboard Canapés

cooked smoked tongue cut to shape on it. Decorate with slices of tiny pickled onions.

20. Roquefort Cheese
Spread a cracker with Roquefort spread. Garnish with ripe olives.

21. Tomato—Egg
Spread crackers with tomato butter. Top with hard boiled egg slices and garnish with a little chopped parsley.

22. Cream Cheese and Radish
Spread cream cheese on rye bread and top with circles of red radishes.

Bacon Canapés (roll-ups)

23. *Checkerboard Canapé*

Alternate 4 slices of bread, half white and half wheat. Spread with your favorite spread or butter. Start with wheat and end with white. Trim off the crusts neatly. Cut into ½ in. slices. Now put the three alternating slices together again using spread or butter. Wrap in waxed paper and refrigerate till well chilled and firm. When ready, slice ½ in. thick and serve.

24. *Canapé of Sardine*

Butter a canapé with sardine butter. Arrange filets of sardine on top. Decorate with anchovy butter.

25. *Canapé À La Mimosa*

Butter round canapé with anchovy butter. Place three small stuffed olives on top to form a triangle and then top with a fourth. Fill in the spaces with anchovy butter and border with mimosa.

26. *Canapé of Smoked Salmon*

Butter a canapé with mustard butter. Top with a piece of smoked salmon and border with a mixture of finely chopped chervil and chives.

27. *Salami Canapé*

Butter a rye canapé lightly with mustard butter. Top with a slice of salami and garnish with a dill pickle slice.

HOT CANAPÉS

28. *Miniature Pizzas*

Using English muffins as a base, split the muffins and place them on a pan, cut side up. Spread each muffin half with 1 tbs. of a prepared tomato sauce, top with a 1 in. cube of Mozzarella cheese. Season with salt, pepper, and oregano, and sprinkle with grated Parmesan cheese and olive oil. Bake at 550° for about 8 min. Serve hot. Allow ½ muffin per person. Variations may be made to the above recipe by simply adding:

(a) Thin slices of uncooked bacon
(b) Thin slices of cooked sausage (Italian style)
(c) One anchovy filet per muffin
(d) Sliced canned or fresh mushrooms
(e) Flaked canned tuna fish
(f) Finely chopped onion or any combination of the above

29. *Bacon Canapé*

Take square cheese-flavored crackers and wrap a half slice of bacon around each cracker. Place on a pan and bake at 450° on each side until the bacon is cooked and crisp. It takes about 12 min. Serve hot.

30. *Cream Cheese and Mushroom Canapé*   (20 pieces)

5 ozs. cream cheese
1 tbs. finely chopped chives

3 ozs. finely chopped mushrooms
1 tbs. butter
1 tsp. Worcestershire sauce
20 crisp onion rounds (crackers)

(1) Combine all the ingredients except the crackers together and blend well.
(2) Spread the mixture on the crackers and sprinkle with paprika. Place on a pan and broil for about 5 min. Garnish with parsley sprigs. Serve hot.

31. *Liverwurst and Chutney Canapé*   (30 slices)

½ lb. liverwurst
½ cup chutney
10 slices of fresh white bread (crusts trimmed)
butter

(1) Mash the skinless liverwurst with a fork and mix in the chutney. On the bread slices, which have been spread with butter, spread on the liverwurst mixture and roll up the bread slices in a jelly roll fashion.
(2) Wrap each roll in waxed paper securely and refrigerate till firm.
(3) Slice roll crosswise three times and toast the thick slices under the broiler.

32. *Asparagus Cheese Canapé*

Take a cooked asparagus spear which is trimmed to the same length as a slice of trimmed fresh white bread. Butter the bread lightly and place the asparagus on one end with a thin slice of process cheese and roll up. Place on a pan, seam side down. Refrigerate until served. When served, brush with melted butter and broil until bread is toasted. Serve as is or sliced into 3 portions.

33. *Country Toast Canapé À La Cal*

Make up a cheese spread by combining ¼ lb. of grated Cheddar cheese, 1 tsp. Worcestershire sauce, 1 tsp. prepared mustard with horse-radish, 2 tbs. milk, dash of Tabasco and paprika.

Work until smooth. Butter trimmed slices of white bread, on one side. Toast under broiler with the buttered side up until lightly browned. Remove from heat and turn over. On the untoasted side, spread the cheese mixture and return to broiler, cheese side up. Broil until hot and bubbly. Slice bread into 3 strips and serve.

34. *Peanut Butter and Onion Canapé*
Slice a small onion crosswise and place a slice on a crisp round cracker. Place a dab of a mixture made of equal parts of catsup and peanut butter (smooth style) and broil under the broiler for a few minutes. Serve hot.

35. *Mozzarella and Anchovy Canapé*
On ½ in. thick slices of crusty Italian bread, lay a slice of Mozzarella cheese, topped with an anchovy filet and some ground black pepper. Place in a hot oven (500°) until cheese is hot and bubbly. Serve hot.

36. *Garlic Bread Canapé*
Slice a French bread in half lengthwise and sprinkle the cut sides with garlic powder, salt, pepper, and olive oil. Place on a pan, seasoned side up and bake in a very hot oven (500°) until it is crisp and toasted. Remove and cut crosswise into 1 in. wide strips. Serve warm.

37. *Tomato and Onion Canapé*
Using an unbaked biscuit round as a base, build up in equal layers a slice of onion, a slice of tomato, a slice of process cheese, and a piece of bacon. Place on a pan and bake at 375° for about 12 min. Serve hot.

38. *Stuffed Rolls*
Hollow out hard French rolls. Fill solidly with a mixture of 3 parts of flavored cream cheese (chive, pimento, blue, etc., and 1 part of butter, well blended). Chill thoroughly and slice just before serving.

39. *Spicy Ham Canapés*

    ½ lb. cooked ham, finely ground
    ½ cup sour cream
    1 tbs. mayonnaise
    1 tsp. curry powder
    ¼ tsp. salt
    a generous dash of onion powder and garlic powder
    2 in. rounds of bread, toasted and buttered

Mix all ingredients well. Spread on the bread rounds. Broil until puffed and brown. Garnish with chopped parsley and a small strip of pimento.

40. *Ham and Egg Canapés*

    1 cup of deviled ham
    2 hard boiled eggs finely chopped
    2 tsp. horse-radish
    toast rounds or crackers

Mix the first 3 ingredients together. Spread on the toast rounds or crackers. Broil very quickly. Garnish with sliced olive, pimento, or as desired.

41. *Zesty Canapé Wheel*

    1 large round loaf of pumpernickel or rye bread
    ⅓ cup chive butter
    1 cup of egg spread
    ⅓ cup red caviar
    ½ cup shrimp spread
    ⅔ cup crab meat spread
    ⅔ cup salmon spread
    ½ cup of stuffed green olives
    chopped parsley

Cut a horizontal ½ in. slice of bread from widest part of the bread. Spread well with the chive butter. Mark four concentric circles by forcing egg spread through a pastry tube to form the rings. Fill the center circle with the caviar and sprinkle with a little chopped parsley. Fill the second ring with shrimp spread, the third ring with crab meat spread, and the fourth ring with salmon spread. Border the wheel with thin overlapping slices of stuffed olives. Cut into wedges but leave intact until ready to serve.

7. Hors D'Oeuvres

QUEEN of the appetizers is the flavorsome, zestful hot hors d'oeuvre, delicious when served straight or with a complementary sauce or dunk. The makings of most of the hot appetizers are already available in the kitchen: bacon, pickles, fruits, canned meats and fish, cheeses, and leftover cooked meats. Sauces can vary from simple prepared mustards or chili sauce to as intricate as time and budget will allow.

Many of the hors d'oeuvres can be prepared in advance and kept frozen until shortly before service. Many others can be prepared at the last moment with a minimum of labor, to satisfy the needs of a spur-of-the-moment party.

The prime ingredients of the hot hors d'oeuvres, as in all successful food preparations, are imagination, an educated touch with seasoning, and a flair for interesting presentation. The delicious flavor of bacon, its convenience as a wrap, and its speed in cooking makes it possible to combine bacon with a great variety of foods to make an excellent finished product.

1. **Bacon Blankets** *

    12 chicken livers
    12 slices of bacon

Cut bacon slices in half. Precook for a few minutes till translucent. Wrap each piece of bacon around half a chicken liver and

---

* Starred hors d'oeuvres may be frozen.

56

fasten with a toothpick. Broil just before serving. Bacon slices
may be wrapped about any of the following and prepared as
above:

Meats

    beef tenderloin tips cubed *
    small sausages *
    cocktail franks or pieces of large frankfurters *
    Bologna or liverwurst cubed *
    small meat balls*
    canned luncheon meat cubed *
    marinated lamb cubed *

Fish

    oysters *
    shrimps *
    scallops *
    crab meat chunks *

Pickles

    stuffed olives
    watermelon rind
    cauliflower
    gherkins

Fruits and Vegetables

    mushroom caps
    potato puffs
    banana chunks
    cantaloupe chunks
    pitted prunes that have been plumped by soaking in sherry *

Cheese
    cubes of American cheese *

Bread
    fingers of bread rolled in grated cheese *

In hamburger-loving America, meat balls of any type find a ready welcome. Meat balls may be served in casserole in their own sauces or may be served on toothpicks with accompanying dips such as prepared mustard, chili sauce, catsup, cheese sauce, chopped pickles, chopped toasted and salted nuts, etc.

2. *Basic Meat Balls* (To Serve with Sauces If Desired) *

    1 lb. ground beef
    2 eggs slightly beaten
    1 cup breadcrumbs moistened
    2 tbs. minced onion
    salt and pepper to taste

Combine ingredients and mix thoroughly. Form into tiny meat balls. Fry quickly in hot fat.

3. *Saucy Meat Balls* *

    1 lb. chopped beef
    ½ cup applesauce
    ½ cup fresh breadcrumbs
    1 lg. egg slightly beaten
    1 onion chopped fine
    salt and pepper to taste
    3 cups prepared tomato sauce (the canned variety is excellent)

Mix all the ingredients but the tomato sauce. Form tiny balls and roll in flour. Brown quickly in hot fat (preferably bacon fat). Transfer meat balls to a casserole. Add tomato sauce. Cover and bake in preheated oven (375°) for 35 to 40 min.

4. *Curried Meat Balls* *

    1 lb. chopped beef
    1 egg slightly beaten
    2 cups flaked coconut
    2 tbs. minced onion

2 tsp. curry powder

1 can cream of mushroom soup diluted with 1 can of milk and 1 can of cream

Mix all the ingredients but the soup. Form tiny meat balls, roll in flour, and brown quickly in hot fat. Transfer drained meat balls to a casserole; cover with diluted cream of mushroom soup. Cover, bake in preheated oven (350°) for 30 min.

Kabobs give an oriental touch to the hors d'oeuvres assortment. They should be miniatures, strung on picks or short skewers, so that they can be managed easily. Use your imagination to combine meats, fish, fruits, and vegetables to please eye and appetite.

5. *Fruited Sausage Kabobs*

pineapple chunks
quarters of brown-and-serve sausage
cocktail onions or small stuffed olives

Alternate above on a pick. Brown on hot griddle before serving.

6. *Combination Kabobs*

Combine the following as desired and cook as above:

chicken livers
bacon slices
prepared sausages and frankfurters of all types
cooked ham cubed
cooked smoked tongue cubed
firm meat balls
tiny onions
tiny cherry tomatoes
green pepper slices
pimento slices
button mushrooms
small pickles or slices of pickles

Combination Kabobs (pineapple, meat ball, olive, and pepper)

    fresh or canned pineapple cubes
    apple cubes
    pickled and spiced fruits
    raw shell fish (oysters, scallops, lobsters, shrimp, crab)
    cubes of parboiled shad roe

Seafood for hors d'oeuvres should be prepared carefully. Fish should be kept well chilled until preparation and service. Seafood is naturally tender and should be cooked only until done. Cooking beyond that point causes a tough and unappetizing product.

7. Batter-Dipped Seafood

    1 lb. large shrimp
    1 cup flour
    1 tsp. baking powder
    ½ tsp. salt

1 tbs. salad oil
¾ cup milk
1 egg well beaten

Shell shrimp, leaving the tail on if preferred. Remove the dark vein from the back of the shrimp. Sift dry ingredients into a bowl. Add oil, milk, and egg. Mix to make a smooth batter. Dip the shrimp in batter. Fry in deep fat (heated to 370°) until golden brown. Serve on picks with sauce such as: tartar, soy, chutney, hot mustard, etc. Shrimp may be butterflied (cut almost through down the back and then flattened) before dipping in batter. Instead of using batter, shrimp may be dipped in any of the following before frying: dry pancake mix; cornstarch, beaten egg, and cornstarch again; flour, beaten egg, and fine dry breadcrumbs.

8. Stuffed Shrimp *

½ lb. fresh lean pork ground
3 scallions finely chopped
2 tbs. celery finely chopped
salt, pepper, and garlic powder to taste
1 lb. med. shrimp
1 egg beaten
dry breadcrumbs

Clean and devein shrimp, leaving the tails attached. Split almost through, opening flat. Sauté pork, scallions, and celery lightly in small amount of butter, until pork loses its pink look. Add seasonings. Spoon a little of this mixture on the shrimp. Fold closed and skewer together with a wood pick. Roll in beaten egg and crumbs. Deep fat fry (375°) until golden brown. These shrimps are delicious served with mustard sauce.

9. Oyster Rockefeller

24 freshly opened oysters on the half-shell
¼ cup butter
1 cup raw spinach finely minced

2 tbs. onion finely minced
2 tbs. parsley finely minced
2 tbs. celery finely minced
½ cup breadcrumbs
few drops of Tabasco sauce
½ tsp. salt

Shuck and drain the oysters. Leave the oyster on the deep half of the shell. Spread rock salt in a shallow baking dish. Place each oyster in the shell on the rock salt. Melt butter; add all ingredients but oysters. Cook, stirring constantly, until the ingredients are soft. Spread the mixture over the oysters. Bake in preheated 400° oven until edges begin to curl. Serve immediately. (Louisiana style adds a few drops of anisette or pernod before baking.)

10. *Oyster Kabob* *

Small oysters make an excellent kabob. Sprinkle them with lemon juice, salt, and pepper and thread on a small skewer with bacon slices and a button mushroom.

11. *Oyster Casino* *

2 doz. oysters
12 slices of bacon cut into halves
½ lb. butter
2 tbs. chopped parsley
10 drops Worcestershire sauce
1 tbs. lemon juice
2 tbs. shallots finely chopped (if available)
3 tbs. green pepper finely chopped
1 tbs. chives chopped
2 tbs. pimento finely chopped
½ tsp. pepper

Make a casino butter by combining all ingredients but the oysters and bacon. Form into a roll, cover with wax paper and refrigerate. Shuck and drain oysters. Place oysters on deep half of shell. Arrange the oysters in the shells in a bed of rock salt spread in a shallow pan. Cover with a slice of the casino butter. Top with a piece of the bacon. Bake in a preheated 400° oven about 10 min. until bacon is cooked.

12. *Broiled Oysters*

> 2 doz. shucked and drained oysters
> 1 cup dried breadcrumbs
> ½ tsp. dried mustard
> ½ tsp. paprika
> ½ tsp. salt
> dash cayenne pepper
> ¼ cup melted butter

Combine the breadcrumbs with the seasonings. Roll the oysters in the crumbs. Place in single layer on greased broiler pan. Sprinkle with half of the butter. Broil quickly until golden brown. Turn; sprinkle with remaining butter. Finish broiling. Serve on picks with lemon.

13. *Crab Meat Rolls* *

> ½ lb. crab meat
> 4 slices of bread (crusts removed) cut into tiny squares
> 2 sm. eggs, slightly beaten
> 1½ tbs. parsley finely chopped
> 1½ tbs. chives finely chopped
> salt and pepper to taste
> 2 tsp. lemon juice

Mix all the ingredients together. Form balls. Roll in flour, beaten eggs, and fine breadcrumbs. Fry in deep fat (350°) until golden brown.

14. *Crab Meat Bacon Rolls and Kabobs* *
Chunks of crab meat combine well with bacon and green peppers to make excellent bacon rolls and kabobs.

15. *Clams Casino*

> 24 cherrystone clams on the half-shell
> casino butter [see Oyster Casino—Hors D'Oeuvres No. 11]
> 12 slices of bacon cut into halves

Set the clams on the half-shell on a bed of rock salt in a shallow pan. Place a slice of casino butter on each clam. Cover with a piece of bacon. Heat in preheated 400° oven until bacon is brown.

16. *Scallop Kabobs* *

Marinate scallops for 30 min. in a mixture of equal packs of dry sherry, soy sauce, and olive oil flavored with chopped fresh ginger and garlic. Alternate on skewers with squares of Canadian bacon. Broil until golden brown.

17. *Fried Scallops* *

Dip scallops in fine dry breadcrumbs, beaten egg, and crumbs. Fry in deep fat 375° until brown. Serve with lemon or sauce.

18. *Scallop Bacon Rolls* *

Scallops may be rolled in bacon and broiled.

19. *Coquille St. Jacques*

> 1 qt. sea scallops
> 1 pt. white wine
> ¼ cup butter
> 1 lb. mushrooms sliced
> 4 green onions finely chopped
> 2 tbs. parsley finely chopped
> 3 tbs. flour
> ¼ cup cream
> breadcrumbs
> butter

Butter small ramekins or shells, if available. Simmer the scallops in the wine for 6 min. Save the liquid and cut the scallops into pieces if they are large. Set aside. Heat the butter in a saucepan. Add the mushrooms and cook for a few minutes. Add the onions and parsley and cook a few minutes longer. Sprinkle in the flour and continue cooking while blending in the flour. Add the liquid in which the scallops were simmered, adding water if necessary to make 2 cups. Stir constantly while the liquid is being slowly added. Stir in the cream and scallops. Fill the shells or ramekins, sprinkle with breadcrumbs, dot with butter. Finish off in broiler until golden brown.

20. Cheese—Rice Balls

>   1 cup nippy cheese
>   2 cups boiled rice
>   prepared mustard
>   horse-radish

Work cheese into tiny balls. Roll lightly in mustard and horse-radish. Roll thoroughly in cooked rice until completely covered. Roll compactly. Fry in deep fat (450°) until golden brown. (Note: The rice should not be rinsed or fluffed after cooking. It will then adhere better.) The cheese—rice balls may be prepared in advance and then reheated in the oven before serving.

21. Cheddar Cheese Puffs

>   1 cup of Cheddar cheese grated
>   1 egg separated
>   ½ tsp. baking powder
>   toast rounds

Beat the egg yolk and white separately. Mix the grated cheese with the egg yolk and baking powder. Fold the beaten egg white into the cheese mixture. Spread on the toast rounds and puff under the broiler until golden brown.

22. Stuffed Mushrooms

>   1 lb. lg. mushrooms
>   ¼ cup butter melted

3 tbs. onion finely chopped
3 tbs. parsley finely chopped
⅓ cup lemon juice
½ tsp. salt
2 cups fine soft breadcrumbs
3 tbs. cream or sherry

Wash, dry, and peel mushrooms if necessary. Chop the stems very fine. Place half the butter in a skillet. Add the onions, chopped mushroom stems, and chopped parsley. Cook 2 or 3 min. Add the crumbs, seasonings, and the cream or sherry to moisten. Place mushroom caps cup side down on baking sheet and brush with melted butter. Broil in preheated broiler for 2 min. Invert, fill with stuffing, brush with butter, and continue broiling for 3 min. (Note: Chopped cooked shrimp, chicken, ham, or bacon may be substituted for part of the breadcrumbs.)

23. *Ham and Biscuits*

2 cups sifted all-purpose flour
3 tsp. baking powder
1 tsp. salt
½ cup shortening
⅔ to ¾ cup milk
6 ozs. of thinly sliced Westphalian ham or Procuitto ham

Sift flour, baking powder, and salt into a bowl. Cut in the shortening with pastry blender or two knives until the mixture is like coarse corn meal. Make a well in the center, pour in half the milk, and mix quickly with a fork. Add additional milk until dough leaves side of bowl and forms a ball around the fork. Turn out in a lightly floured board. Knead gently 7 or 8 times. Roll out, not more than ½ inch thick. Cut into tiny biscuits, not larger than a half-dollar in size. Place on ungreased baking pan. Brush the tops of the biscuits with a little milk. Bake about 12 min. in preheated 450° oven. While the biscuits are still *piping hot*, split them, butter, and place a small slice of the ham between the biscuit halves. Serve hot and generously. (Prepared biscuit mix may be used. Biscuits may be flavored *delicately* with a *little* paprika or a *little* very finely chopped parsley, finely chopped chives, or a little onion powder. Thinly sliced chicken may be used with the ham or instead of the ham. Thinly sliced smoked tongue may be used instead of ham.)

24. *Quick Pastry Sticks* *

¼ cup salt butter
¼ cup cream cheese
1 cup flour
2 tbs. grated strong Cheddar
2 tbs. crumbled Blue cheese
1½ tbs. caraway seeds
garlic powder

Knead thoroughly. Divide into thirds. Add grated strong Cheddar to one third, crumbled Blue cheese to one third, and caraway seeds to one third. Refrigerate 20 min. Roll out ⅜ in. thick. Sprinkle the caraway portion with garlic powder. Cut into fingers. Bake in preheated 450° oven 6 to 7 min.

25. *Piroshki*

1½ cups flour
1½ tsp. baking powder
1 egg
¼ cup shortening (chicken fat can be used)
pinch of salt
¼ cup water approximately
¾ cup cooked beef (leftover pot roast is excellent) ⎤
2 broiled chicken livers
1 onion, sliced and fried   ⎬ filling
1 egg
salt and pepper   ⎦

Run meat, liver, and onion through food chopper; add the egg and seasonings. Combine the flour, baking powder, egg, shortening, and salt. Add just enough water to form a soft dough about ⅛ in. thick and cut into 3 in. circles. Place a scant table-spoon of mixture on each circle; fold the circle in half and pinch the edges together. Place on greased baking sheet and bake in preheated oven 400° until brown (about 30 min.). A flaky pie crust dough or a rich raised dough may be used instead of the dough in the above recipe.

Mushrooms make a delicious filling for the piroshki:

> 1 lb. of mushrooms chopped fine
> 6 scallions chopped fine
> ¼ cup butter
> salt and pepper to taste
> 2 tbs. flour
> ⅓ cup sour cream

Heat the butter, add the scallions and mushrooms, and cook gently for 5 min. Add seasoning, sprinkle with flour, add sour cream. Cook until thickened. Cool and proceed with filling and baking the circles of dough.

Miniature turnovers, tartlets, and barquettes (boat-shaped tarts) make enticing and delicious appetizers. A good flaky pie crust—or even a good pie-crust mix—makes an excellent product. However, puff paste is so superior that it is worth the extra care involved in its making. It is for this reason that the following recipe for puff pastry is offered. Once mastered it can be used for many dishes.

26. *Puff Pastry*

> 2 cups of sweet butter (1 lb.)
> 4 cups of all-purpose flour (1 lb.)
> ½ tsp. salt
> 1¼ cups of ice water

Work the butter well, kneading it until all the water has been worked out. Form the butter into a flat rectangular cake. Sprin-kle 2 tbs. of the flour onto the butter, wrap in wax paper, and refrigerate. Sift the remaining flour and salt into a bowl or onto a pastry board or marble slab. Form a well in the center. Add the water gradually, working the flour and water with the finger-tips to form a firm dough. Knead well. Roll the dough into an oblong, 1 in. thick. Place the cake of butter in the center. Fold ⅓ of the dough over the center third. Now fold the other third over the center, making 3 layers and covering the butter completely. (This process of rolling and folding is called a "turn.") Now repeat the folding process with the oblong you have formed to make a square. Chill for 20 min. Roll out again, forming an oblong ½ in. thick and 3 times as long as it is wide. Fold in thirds as already described. Turn the dough so that an end faces you. Roll and fold again. Refrigerate for 20 min. Repeat this process another 2 times, making 2 turns each time. Refrigerate for 15 min. The dough is now ready to use.

Fillings for Turnovers, Tartlets, and Barquettes

Crab meat: mix shredded crab meat with seasoning and a little sweet cream until smooth and at proper consistency
Lobster or shrimp Newburgh: Cut seafood into small pieces
Curried shrimp or crab meat
Curried mushrooms
Chopped chicken, ham, and mushrooms in cream

27. *Cheese and Bacon Balls*

> 1 lb. sharp cheese
> ⅓ cup mayonnaise
> ½ lb. bacon

Fry the bacon until crisp. Drain well and crumble fine. Grate the cheese and blend with the mayonnaise. Form into tiny balls and roll in the crumbled bacon. Serve on picks.

28. *Asparagus Rolls*

Marinate asparagus in French dressing. Spread thin slices of ham, smoked tongue, or dried beef with a light layer of mayonnaise and roll around the asparagus.

29. *Miniature Tartare Steaks*

  1 lb. lean round finely ground
  1 egg
  1 tsp. Worcestershire sauce
  salt and pepper
  chopped parsley
  very small onions sliced thin

Mix the meat, egg, and seasonings. Form small balls and place each ball on a slice of onion. Sprinkle lightly with parsley.

30. *Salmon Rolls*

  ½ lb. cream cheese
  ¼ lb. butter
  2 tsp. lemon juice
  1 lb. smoked salmon sliced very thin
  sweet gherkins

Cream the cream cheese, butter, and lemon juice. Place the salmon slices close together on wax paper to form a strip 6 to 7 in. long and flatten with a knife. Spread the mix on the strip. Trim the ends from a gherkin. Place the gherkin at one end of the salmon strip. Lift the wax paper to start the roll, then roll up the strip, wrap in wax paper, and refrigerate. Cut slices and serve on a cracker or toast round.

31. *Chopped Chicken Liver Mold* *

  1 lb. chicken livers
  ¼ cup chicken fat
  1 cup onion diced
  2 tbs. parsley chopped
  1 tsp. salt
  pepper to taste
  3 hard cooked eggs
  3 tbs. butter (optional)

Sauté seasoned (salt and pepper) chicken livers and onions in chicken fat. When cooked, put through a food chopper with eggs. Mix well in bowl and add parsley and butter if desired. Pack in greased mold and refrigerate. To serve, immerse mold quickly in water and then turn out on platter. Add garnishes.

32. *Pâté Maison*

    2 lbs. chicken or calf liver
    ⅛ lb. chicken fat
    ⅛ lb. butter or shortening
    ½ cup chopped onion
    1 tbs. salt
    ¼ tsp. pepper
    ¼ tsp. thyme
    1 bay leaf
    3 tbs. cognac

Sauté livers and onions in fat and butter until browned, stirring frequently, together with seasonings, bay leaf, and thyme. Cook about 5 min. Remove from stove and cool. Pass through fine knife (after discarding thyme and bay leaf) of food chopper twice. Mix in cognac. Wrap in wax paper and refrigerate. Serve on hot buttered toast or croutons.

33. *Stuffed Celery*

    ⅔ lb. cream cheese
    ⅓ lb. Blue cheese
    ¼ lb. butter
    1 tsp. lemon juice
    1 tsp. Worcestershire sauce

Put Blue cheese through a fine strainer. Blend in softened cream cheese, butter, and seasonings. Mix well. Trim and clean celery, removing leaves from all but the smallest pieces. Fill a pastry bag with the cheese mixture and force through a star tube into the celery. Dust lightly with paprika if desired. Refrigerate until ready to serve.

34. *Stuffed Pickled Beets*
Hollow tiny pickled beets slightly. Fill through a pastry tube with any of the desired butters or spreads mentioned in earlier chapters. (Note: Many raw vegetables can be used to make delicious and attractive cups for butters and spreads. Score cucumber with a fork or peel with a fluted knife. Cut slices a scant inch thick, hollow out, and stuff. Carrots, too, may be cut in slices and hollowed out. Tiny cherry tomatoes and red radishes—with a little of the stem left on—also make attractive cups.)

35. *Stuffed Artichoke Hearts*
Stuff drained canned artichoke hearts with caviar; sprinkle with a little finely chopped onion and serve with lemon wedges.

36. *Stuffed Brussel Sprouts*
Cook brussel sprouts until just tender. Chill. Hollow out carefully and fill with deviled ham or chopped smoked tongue moistened with a little chili sauce.

37. *Sherried Prunes*
Soak jumbo prunes in sherry till plump. Stuff the prune with softened cream cheese and garnish by inserting an almond into the cream cheese so that most of the almond is exposed.

38. *Figs and Ham*
Wrap a thin slice of Westphalian or procuitto ham around a fresh fig. Fasten with a pick and serve with a wedge of lemon or lime.

39. *Bananas and Ham*
Bananas dipped in lemon juice and wrapped in ham are also delicious.

HOT QUICKIES

Quickly prepared from pantry supplies:

(1) Frozen ravioli, defrosted and carefully dried, deep-fat fried at 370° until brown. Drained and salted.

(2) Frozen fish sticks, cut into bite-size pieces and heated. Serve on picks with a "dunk" sauce or lemon wedges.

(3) Canned Vienna sausage or chunks of canned frankfurters, dipped in pancake batter (made from a mix), and deep-fat fried at 370° until brown. Serve on pick with prepared mustard.

(4) Canned deviled ham (or canned corned beef chopped and mixed with a little prepared mustard) spread between thin slices of bread. This sandwich then cut into small rounds or squares, dipped into egg beaten with a little milk, and fried in hot butter.

(5) Frozen or canned French fried onions, heated and served.

(6) Canned tuna or sardines mixed with a little mayonnaise, salt, pepper, and onion salt until creamy. Spread on crackers and quickly broiled.

(7) Clam fritters, made by combining drained canned minced clams with pancake mix, beaten egg, and a little milk; then dropped from a teaspoon onto hot fat in a skillet and fried until brown.

(8) Tiny puffs made from prepared cream-puff mix and filled at the last moment with a little hot creamed chicken or seafood.

(9) Breakfast sausages, cut in half and pecan-half stuffed into each piece of sausage, baked at 400° until brown and crisp. Served on picks.

(10) Frozen french fries sprinkled with Parmesan cheese while heating.

8. The Buffet

FOR the large private cocktail party that often runs on well past the dinner hour, or for that bit of suburbia, "The Sunday Night Supper Party," the long buffet table predominates. Attractive center arrangements of fruit baskets help conserve space and add colorful scope for imaginative planning.

1. **Proscuitto and Melon**

   Cut slices of pared cantaloupe or honeydew melon and top each slice with a paper thin piece of proscuitto. Keep chilled until served. Serve with a wedge of lemon. An average, medium-sized cantaloupe should yield about 12 slices of the appropriate size for this dish.

2. **Artichokes À La Grecque**   (20 portions)

   > 20 sm. artichokes
   > 1 pt. water
   > 4 ozs. olive oil
   > juice of 3 lemons
   > 12 pepper corns crushed
   > ⅛ tsp. thyme
   > 1 bay leaf
   > salt to taste
   > 10 coriander seeds
   > 10 fennel seeds crushed

(1) Remove the outer coarse leaves of the artichokes and trim the coarse outer portion of the tail and crown.

(2) Boil the artichokes for 10 min. in water to which a few drops of vinegar have been added.

(3) Drain the artichokes, cool them in fresh water, and then drain them again.

(4) Make a marinade by placing in a saucepan and boiling for 15 min. the water, lemon juice, olive oil, and spices. After the 15 min., add the artichokes to the marinade and cook until tender.

(5) Cool the artichokes in the marinade and serve cold with some marinade poured over.

3. *Rollatini of Mortadella*

Have mortadella sliced a little thicker than usual and spread 1 tbs. of this mixture on each slice. For every 6 ozs. of cream cheese used, add the grated, drained pulp of a large cucumber, 1 tbs. chopped chives, and a few drops of lemon juice. Whip all ingredients together. Roll the mortadella up, jelly roll fashion, and place on a pan, seam side down. Refrigerate until cheese mixture hardens. When ready to be served, cut at an angle into 1 in. thick slices.

4. *Artichoke Hearts in Olive Oil*   (20 portions)

20 small artichokes
½ cup lemon juice
3 cups dry white wine
3 tbs. wine vinegar
8 bay leaves
12 pepper corns crushed (white)
4 cloves (whole)
½ lemon cut into thin slices
olive oil as needed

(1) Remove outer leaves of the artichokes, and trim the coarse outer portion of the tail and crown. Dip into the lemon juice.

(2) Place the artichokes in a saucepan with the remaining lemon juice, vinegar, white wine, cloves and lemon slices, and ½ the quantity of bay leaves and pepper corns.

(3) Bring to a boil and cook until the artichokes are tender. Allow to cool in the liquor.

(4) After the artichokes are cool, drain them thoroughly and place them in a jar with the rest of the bay leaves and pepper corns and cover with olive oil. Allow them to sit in the olive oil at least 3 days before serving.

5. *Quiche Lorraine*   (20 portions)

> 12 slices of crisp-cooked drained bacon crumbled
> 1 cup natural Swiss cheese cut in fine strips
> 4 eggs
> 1½ cups heavy cream
> ½ cup beef stock
> ½ tsp. salt
> ½ tsp. ground white pepper
> pinch each of nutmeg, cayenne, sugar
> 5 Ritz crackers crumbled fine

(1) In an 11 in. pie tin, which has been lined with an uncooked pie crust dough, sprinkle the crumbled Ritz crackers along the bottom.

(2) Follow this with the bacon and then the Swiss cheese.

(3) In a bowl, mix until just blended, the eggs, cream, stock, and seasonings. Pour this mixture into the pie shell.

(4) Bake in a preheated oven at 400° for about 15 min. Reduce the heat to 325° and continue baking for about 20 min. or until a silver knife inserted in the center comes out clean. Serve hot and cut into wedges.

Pie Crust Recipe

> 6 ozs. all-purpose flour
> ½ tsp. salt
> ½ cup shortening (hydrogenated type)
> ¼ cup ice water

(1) Sift flour and salt together.
(2) Cut in shortening and work quickly with fingers until it crumbles.
(3) Add water and blend in with a fork.
(4) Shape into a ball and refrigerate for about 1 hr.
(5) Roll out on a floured board and fit into pie tin. Flute the edges decoratively and prick the bottom of the shell with the tines of a fork. Refrigerate for about ½ hr. more. Then use as needed.

6. Cream Cheese Sandwich Loaf

1 large pullman loaf of bread unsliced
2 large tomatoes cut in about 12 slices or as needed
Chicken Salad Spread (see No. 7 following)
Ham Salad Spread (No. 8)
Egg Salad Spread (No. 9)
Sharp Cheese Spread (No. 10)
Cream Cheese Spread (No. 11)

(1) Trim crusts off the top, sides and bottom of the pullman loaf. Then carefully slice the bread into 5 equal slices, cut *lengthwise*.
(2) On the bottom slice, spread about ½ in. of the Sharp Cheese Spread. On the second slice, spread some Ham Salad. Top this with the tomato slices and then top the tomatoes with more Ham Salad.
(3) On the third slice, use the Chicken Salad and on the fourth slice, the Egg Salad.
(4) Then place the slices back on top of each other in their proper sequence and top off the "sandwich" with the fifth slice.
(5) Even off the edges and round the top slices.
(6) Frost the sides and top with the Cream Cheese Spread. Decorate the sides and edges with the spread applied from a pastry bag using a fine star tube.
(7) Garnish the loaf with sliced radishes, watercress, and parsley. Refrigerate overnight.

7. *Chicken Salad Spread*

1 cup pureed cooked chicken or turkey meat
½ cup finely minced celery
4 tbs. sweet relish
4 tbs. mayonnaise
salt and pepper

Blend together and refrigerate until needed.

8. *Ham Salad Spread*

1 cup pureed cooked or canned ham
4 tbs. finely minced green pepper
1 tbs. prepared mustard
2 tbs. finely minced onion
4 tbs. mayonnaise
salt and pepper

Blend together and refrigerate until needed.

9. *Egg Salad Spread*

4 hard cooked eggs pureed
4 tbs. finely minced ripe olives
1 tbs. prepared mustard
4 tbs. mayonnaise
salt and pepper

Blend together and refrigerate until needed.

10. *Sharp Cheese Spread*

½ lb. natural sharp cheese
4 ozs. hot water

Soften up the cheese and add the hot water. Mix well, to a spreading consistency. Add more water if needed.

11. *Cream Cheese Spread*

> 1½ lbs. cream cheese
> 1 cup med. cream (more if needed)

Blend together. If it does not spread easily enough, add more cream.

12. *Potato Salad*   (20 portions)

> 20 med. potatoes cooked, cooled, and diced
> 4½ cups diced celery
> 1 cup finely diced scallions
> 1 cup finely diced onions
> 4 cups mayonnaise
> 4 tbs. white distilled vinegar
> 3 tbs. prepared mustard
> 1 tsp. celery salt
> salt and pepper to taste
> 1 cup sliced radishes

Combine all ingredients together. Toss lightly and refrigerate until served. Garnish with parsley, tomato wedges, or stuffed olives.

13. *Macaroni Salad*   (20 portions)

Follow the Potato Salad recipe, but omit the potatoes and substitute 5 lbs. of cooked and cooled macaroni.

14. *Cucumber Salad with Sour Cream*   (20 portions)

> 10 large cucumbers (pared and thinly sliced)
> 1 tbs. salt
> ½ tsp. ground white pepper
> 8 tbs. finely minced chives
> 3 cups sour cream
> 5 tbs. lemon juice

Blend salt, pepper, lemon juice, chives, and sour cream. Add cucumber slices and refrigerate at least 40 min. before serving.

15. *Waldorf Salad*   (20 portions)

  7 cups of dried unpared red apples
  6 tbs. lemon juice
  1 tbs. granulated sugar
  1½ cups walnuts (rough cut)
  3 cups celery thinly sliced
  1½ cups mayonnaise
  1 cup raisins (soak in very hot water for 20 min. before
  using)

Toss all ingredients together, blending well. Refrigerate until served.

16. *Sliced Tomato Salad*

Cut into wedges any desired amount of firm ripe tomatoes. Lay on a platter and sprinkle generously with barely crushed cloves of garlic. Add olive oil, salt, pepper, basil, and oregano. Add some thin slices of green hot peppers and a few thin slices of onion rings. Allow to marinate for about 2 hrs. Serve as is, chilled and garnished with parsley sprigs.

17. *Coleslaw*   (20 portions)

  15 cups finely shredded cabbage
  2 tbs. salt
  1 tsp. ground white pepper
  1 tbs. celery salt
  6 tbs. sugar
  3 tbs. chopped pimento
  1½ tbs. finely chopped onion
  2½ cups mayonnaise
  5 tbs. olive oil
  ¾ cup finely sliced green pepper

Blend all ingredients well, mixing thoroughly. Chill until served.

18. *Caesar Salad*   (20 portions)

 3 cloves garlic pureed
 1 head iceberg lettuce
 1 head chicory
 ½ head Boston lettuce
 ½ head escarole
 1 bunch watercress
 3 cups croutons
 6 ozs. anchovy filets
 8 lg. tomatoes diced
 3 eggs raw and beaten
 1¼ cups grated Parmesan cheese
 2 tsp. fresh ground black pepper
 1½ tsp. salt
 ¼ cup lemon juice
 3 tbs. Worcestershire sauce
 1½ cups French Dressing (see below)

(1) Rub pureed garlic on salad bowl.
(2) Place crisp washed greens in bowl.
(3) Add all other ingredients and toss lightly (but thoroughly) to mix well.

French Dressing   (1½ cups approx.)

 1 cup olive oil
 ⅓ cup cider vinegar
 ⅛ cup water
 1 tsp. salt
 ½ tsp. paprika
 1 tsp. sugar
 ¼ tsp. English mustard
 1 tbs. Worcestershire sauce
 1 clove garlic
 1 dash Tabasco

(1) Whip all ingredients together thoroughly and allow to marinate together several hours before using.
(2) Shake well before serving.

19. *Crab Meat Stuffed Avocados*   (20 portions)

    10 ripe avocados (peeled, pitted, and sprinkled with lemon)
    2½ cups mayonnaise
    1 cup finely minced pimento
    2½ cups finely minced celery
    1 tsp. Tabasco
    1 tsp. Worcestershire sauce
    2 tbs. lemon juice
    7 cups crab meat (backfin lump style)
    salt and white pepper to taste

(1) Blend together all the ingredients except the crab meat and avocados.
(2) Fold the crab meat in carefully, taking care that it does not break.
(3) Fill the cavity of each avocado half with the crab meat mixture. Refrigerate until served.

20. *Bread Sticks and Proscuitto*   (20 portions)

    20 short bread sticks
    20 slices proscuitto

(1) Fold proscuitto slices in half (long ends) so that they resemble slices of bacon.
(2) Rap each bread stick with a proscuitto slice, so that the proscuitto comes half-way up the bread stick. Arrange decoratively, garnished with parsley sprigs.

21. *Salmon Mousse*   (for 1 qt. mold, 5 servings)

    1 tbs. gelatin
    2 ozs. cold water
    4 ozs. hot chicken stock
    ½ cup mayonnaise
    1 tbs. finely minced onion

3 cups flaked salmon (cooked)
½ cup whipped cream
1 tbs. cider vinegar
salt and pepper to taste
1 tbs. Worcestershire sauce

Soften gelatin in the cold water. Add the hot chicken stock to the gelatin. Allow it to dissolve and let cool. Add all other ingredients, except the salmon and cream, and let them set in the refrigerator until thick. Remove from the refrigerator and beat until light and foamy. Fold in the salmon and the whipped cream and pour into the mold. Chill until firmly set.

22. *Deviled Eggs* (20 portions)

10 hard boiled eggs
½ cup mayonnaise
¼ cup softened butter
½ tsp. salt
⅛ tsp. white pepper
½ tsp. prepared mustard
2 tsp. pureed onion
¼ tsp. English mustard
dash Worcestershire and Tabasco

(1) Peel and halve the eggs lengthwise.
(2) Remove the yolks and pass through a fine sieve.
(3) Combine sieved yolks and the rest of the ingredients. Mix thoroughly.
(4) Refill the whites with this filling, using a pastry bag and a fine star tube for a decorative effect. Top each filling with a small piece of pimento or black olive or a sprinkle of paprika. Serve chilled.

23. *Assorted Antipasto*
Prepare platters, decoratively laid out, using some or all of the following items:

Sliced proscuitto salami, mortadella, pepperoni, provolone, Mozzarella, tunafish, anchovies, sardines, artichoke hearts, tomatoes, scallions, lettuce, olives, celery, radishes, finocchio, pimentos, salted capers, cucumbers, and carrot sticks.

24. *Crab Meat Remick*

1 lb. lump crab meat
1 tsp. powdered mustard
1 tsp. tarragon vinegar
few drops of Tabasco sauce
1½ cups mayonnaise
½ cup chili sauce
½ tsp. celery salt
½ tsp. paprika

(1) Line buttered ramekins or tart shells with crab meat.
(2) Heat in moderate oven.
(3) Combine all other ingredients. Blend well.
(4) Spread over warmed crab meat.
(5) Heat in oven.
(6) Finish under broiler to glaze lightly.

25. *Mushrooms À La Grecque*

2 lbs. mushrooms
1 cup water
1 cup vinegar
1 cup olive oil
1 clove garlic
1 stalk celery diced
2 med. onions sliced
few sprigs parsley
½ tsp. thyme
1 bay leaf
8 peppercorns
1 tsp. coriander seed

(1) Wash mushrooms. Do not peel. Cut large ones to bite size.
(2) Combine all other ingredients in large pot and bring to a boil. Simmer 5 min.
(3) Add the mushrooms; cook 10 min.
(4) Cool and refrigerate overnight in liquid.

26. *Veal Sauté*   (6 servings)

    2 lbs. veal sliced thinly
    3 tbs. salad oil
    3 tbs. butter
    1 tsp. salt
    ¼ tsp. pepper
    2 tbs. flour
    1 cup white wine
    ¼ tsp. garlic salt
    ½ cup minced onions
    1 cup sliced mushrooms
    12 sm. white onions cooked
    1 tbs. lemon juice

(1) Season with salt and pepper and dredge in flour.
(2) Cook at moderately high heat in oil and butter until browned lightly.
(3) Pour wine over meat.
(4) Add garlic salt, minced onions, and lemon juice.
(5) Bring to a boil and add mushrooms and onions.
(6) Cook 5 min.
(7) Sprinkle with chopped parsley and serve.

27. *Paella*

    2 frying chickens, 2 lbs. each, cut into portions
    ½ cup olive oil
    ½ lb. veal cubed
    ½ lb. choriza (Spanish hot sausage) or pork cubed
    1 lg. onion chopped fine
    2 lg. sweet peppers, cut into strips

4 lg. fresh tomatoes peeled and diced
3 cups of long-grain rice
4 cups of chicken stock
1½ tsp. salt
2 cloves garlic peeled
½ tsp. saffron
1 lb. peeled deveined shrimp
1 lb. lobster meat
10 frozen artichoke hearts
1 pkg. frozen peas
24 sm. clams
12 mussels

Make chicken stock by cooking chicken necks, wing tips and giblets in 4½ cups water, salted. Heat olive oil in a heavy pan. Brown the chicken, veal, sausage, onion, and red peppers. Add the tomatoes and simmer 10 min. Add the rice and cook 5 min. Add the stock and the salt. Make a paste of the saffron and garlic and stir into the mixture. Add the shrimp, lobster meat, and artichoke hearts. Cook for 20 min. Add the peas and cook 5 min. longer. Transfer to a preheated 350° oven. Arrange the well-scrubbed clams and mussels on the contents of the casserole. Bake 10 min.

28. **Maurice Salad**   (by Chef Aime Petran, Hotel New Yorker)
This is one of the most delicious of mixed-salad bowls and will honor any buffet table:

julienne of lettuce
chopped dill pickle
julienne of tomatoes
ham, tongue, imported Swiss cheese
white turkey and egg

Dressing

Paprika mixed with a little vinegar and plain mayonnaise. Season to taste.

29. *Guacamole*

    1 clove garlic
    ¼ tsp. salt
    1 ripe avocado
    ¼ tsp. chili powder
    2 tsp. minced onion
    2 tsp. lemon juice
    1 tomato diced

Rub a bowl with cut garlic clove. Discard garlic. Mash avocado in bowl and add all other ingredients. Serve on lettuce leaf. Garnish with pimento. (Note: This mixture can be used also as a dip or spread. If desired, this may be formed in a mold and garnished in a decorative fashion for the buffet.)

9. Salute to "The Lobster"

MIKE Linz and Stan Fuchs, second generation coproprietors of The Lobster, one of New York's most famous seafood houses, have graciously permitted the use of some of their most succulent recipes taken from their own delightful book, *The Lobster's Fine Kettle of Fish*.

Skewered shrimp make wonderful quick appetizers in any one of these combinations:

(1) Skewer cooked shrimp with avocado chunks.
(2) Arrange shrimp alternately with artichoke hearts.
(3) Alternate shrimp with pearl onions.
(4) Skewer cooked shrimp and tiny cocktail sausages on picks. Brown with butter and broil until thoroughly heated.

One may also spear both ends of a cooked shrimp on a pick, pressing the ends together to form a little hollow to hold a bit of the following filling:

> 2 tbs. mayonnaise
> 1 tbs. fresh dill minced (parsley or tarragon may be sub-
> stituted)
> dash of Tabasco sauce
> ¼ tsp. grated onion

Garnish each filled shrimp boat with a dot of pimento or a minute sprig of greenery.

1. *Crab Toasts*

> 1 can crab meat drained and flaked
> ½ cup finely chopped celery
> ½ green pepper finely minced
> 1 pimento chopped
> ½ cup mayonnaise

Combine the ingredients and spread mixture on thin rounds of toast that are thoroughly cool.

2. *Crab and Ripe Olive Canapés*
Flake 1 sm. can drained crab meat, and add to it ½ cup very finely chopped celery, ¼ cup chopped ripe olives, 1 tbs. lemon juice, and 2 tsp. finely chopped green pepper. Moisten with mayonnaise. Spread on paper-thin slices of party rye bread.

3. *Creamed Crab Canapés*

> ½ lb. crab meat
> ½ lb. finely chopped sautéed mushrooms
> 1 tbs. chopped pimento
> 1 cup well-seasoned cream sauce
> 2 tbs. sherry

Heap the mixture on the untoasted side of rounds of toast, sprinkle with fine dry breadcrumbs, and broil lightly. (The crumbs may be dotted with butter if preferred.)

4. *Crab—Caviar Canapés*
Mash crab to a paste and arrange it in a border around the edges of tiny rounds of bread which have been toasted on one side (the toasted side goes down). Fill the center with caviar after first toasting the canapés for 1 or 2 min. Serve promptly.

Finely chopped cooked shrimp, devastatingly seasoned or set off by the cool tang of watercress, sautéed and curried or broiled in an onion-cheese mixture, are the basis for other cocktail hour delights:

5. *Shrimp Toast*

Cream 1 stick butter until very light and then fold into it ¼ lb. finely chopped cooked shrimp and a dash of Tabasco sauce. Spread on tiny rounds of very hot toast just before serving. Garnish with chopped fresh dill.

6. *Shrimp—Cress Canapés*

   ¾ cup finely chopped cooked shrimp
   2 tbs. mayonnaise
   2 tbs. chili sauce
   ½ tsp. grated onion
   ¼ tsp. celery salt
   1 tsp. lemon juice
   leaves from 1 bunch of watercress chopped (save stems for use in salads)

Combine ingredients and spread on rounds of Melba toast.

7. *Curried Shrimp Canapés*

Sauté shrimp in butter (either cooked or raw shrimp may be used, but the latter will require longer cooking). Sprinkle lightly with curry powder and dry mustard. Place each shrimp on a tiny toast square and garnish with paprika.

8. *Hot Shrimp Fingers*

Soften ½ lb. grated sharp Cheddar cheese and ¼ lb. butter at room temperature about 3 hrs. Cream together and add ¼ cup grated onion, 1 tsp. Worcestershire sauce, ¼ cup lemon juice, and ½ tsp. paprika. Stir in 2 cups finely chopped cooked shrimp. Spread on split finger rolls (or toast fingers), garnish each with a tiny whole cooked shrimp, and broil 3 in. from the flame until cheese is brown and bubbling.

9. *Dill—Sour Cream Sauce* (Dip)

   1½ cups commercial sour cream
   1 tbs. freshly minced dill

a grating of onion
½ cup grated hard boiled egg
1 tsp. dry mustard
½ tsp. celery salt
cayenne

Combine ingredients. Serve with either hot or cold seafood.

10. *Thousand Island Sauce*

1 cup mayonnaise
2 tbs. chopped stuffed olives
1 tbs. finely chopped green pepper
2 tbs. chili sauce
1 tbs. minced chives (or green onion)
½ cup cream whipped

Fold mayonnaise into whipped cream and then add other ingredients.

FISH FILLIPS

Here are garnishes galore to enhance and complement the flavor and appearance of many fish dishes. Start with these, then go as far as your own imagination and ingenuity will carry you.

Anchovies: Whole, rolled, or paste.
Bacon: Broiled, whole or crumbled.
Bananas: Sautéed halves.
Boiled beets: Hollowed out as cups for tartare sauce or horse-radish.
Butter balls: Anchovy, lemon, parsley, chives, dill, tarragon, etc.
Carrots: Curls made by cutting raw carrots lengthwise in paper-thin slices with vegetable peeler. Roll strips around index finger and secure with a bit of toothpick. Crisp on ice and then remove picks. A sprig of herb may be tucked in each ring.
Celery fans: Made by cutting ribs of celery into 2 in. lengths and making a number of parallel cuts in one end almost to center. Crisp on ice to make fringe curl.
Chives chopped.
Croutons: Tiny cubes cut from stale bread (crust removed) and fried in butter. (Especially good on broiled fish.)

Cucumbers: **Slices** from unpared scored (with tines of fork) cucumbers. **Boats** for salad dressings made by hollowing out cucumbers. **Stuffed slices** made by removing center of cucumber with apple corer and then stuffing center with cream cheese filling. **Balls** made by cutting large cucumbers with a French vegetable ball cutter (marinate in French dressing and then roll in paprika or chopped herbs). **Tulips** made by removing ends of cucumber and cutting remaining portion into 2 in. lengths, then cutting 6 triangular sections down from cut edge to make petals. Remove remaining seed, leaving a ¼ in. wall. Tuck a bit of carrot inside center. Chill.

Dill sprigs or chopped.

Green pepper: Finely chopped, either raw or sautéed. Rings to be filled with finely chopped onion or tiny pearl onions—or fit a thin slice of lemon inside each and sprinkle with minced parsley. Peppers may be parboiled 3 min. in boiling salted water prior to cutting in rings, if less flavor is desired.

Hard boiled eggs: Grated, sliced, or cut in wedges.

Lemons: **Quarter-inch slices** from which seed and white membrane have been removed, with herb spray tucked in center. **Pinked baskets** filled with tartare sauce. **Slices with edges pinked** and dipped in finely chopped parsley. **Slices** with one-half sprinkled with paprika. (Cover one side with wax paper while sprinkling paprika.) **Quarters** with membrane edge (center) dipped in paprika (dipping first in melted butter will make paprika adhere better). **Halves** with notched edges and herb sprig in center.

Mushrooms: Sautéed whole, sliced, or chopped.

Olives: Stuffed, sliced, or chopped; or whole ones wrapped with a bit of bacon fastened with pick and French fried.

Onions: Thin **rings,** or chopped. **Whole** pearl onions sprinkled over fish or in sauce.

Oranges: Thin fresh slices, or thin slices dipped in batter and French fried (they always draw comments).

Parsley: Sprigs or minced. (Try them sautéed and French fried too.)

Pickled beets: Tiny whole ones or slices of large ones.

Pickles: Whole, sliced, or chopped. (Dill pickle is especially good on fish.)

Pimentos: Chopped, slivered, or cut in designs.

Pineapple: Rings, grilled, sautéed, or fried in batter. Half-rings seem to lend themselves to more attractive arrangements than whole ones.

Radishes: **Roses** made by cutting thin slices from root end and then cutting sides in thin petals. Leave on part of green stem if fresh and crisp. Crisp to make open. **Bouquets** made by tucking two or three short sprigs of watercress around radish rose (insert pick if rose has no stem) and inserting "nosegay" into cucumber ring. **Slices. Fans** made by laying radish on side and cutting into very thin slices but not all the way through. Chill to open.

Spiced prunes: Cook as usual, but add stick cinnamon and lemon slices. These go especially well with shellfish.

Tomatoes: **Whole** baked sm. ones. **Grilled** halves or slices. Fresh **slices**— but these can get monotonous.

Truffles: Chopped, or cut into designs.

Watercress: **Sprigs** or chopped leaves. (Save stems for salads.) **Bouquets** made by tucking sprigs in raw carrot rings.

11. *Shrimp—Oyster Jambalaya*   (6 to 8 servings)

    2 lbs. raw shrimp shelled
    2 doz. oysters
    salt and pepper
    3 tbs. butter
    1 tbs. flour
    4 cups shrimp stock (or other)
    6 spring onions finely chopped
    1 green pepper seeded and chopped
    1 cup finely chopped celery
    1 cup chopped cooked ham
    2 cups chopped cooked chicken (bite-size pieces)
    6 cups cooked rice

Cook shrimp in salted boiling water 3 to 5 min., or until they have turned pink. Drain (save stock). Melt butter and stir in flour. Add hot stock slowly, stirring constantly until sauce is smooth (it will be thin). Add onion, green pepper, and celery, and simmer 5 min., or until vegetables are half-tender. Add oysters and simmer until their edges begin to curl. Add shrimp, ham, chicken, and heat thoroughly. Season with pepper. Fold rice into mixture, and heat through. Pour into a hot shallow serving bowl. Garnish with whole shrimp and parsley sprigs.

12. *Shrimp Sarapico*   (individual serving)
Make a paste of 2 ozs. of cream cheese, 2 ozs. of Roquefort cheese, and 1 chopped pimento. Spread the paste on a piece

of aluminum foil about 12 in. square. Place ¼ lb. of cleaned raw shrimp on the paste, and top with two thin slices of lemon. Close the aluminum foil bag by pinching the top together. Bake 30 min. in a 400° oven. To serve Shrimp Sarapico, place each hot foil bag on a plate, and let each guest open his own. (Oh, the fragrance that wafts upward when the bag is opened.)

13. *Scalloped Lobster*   (6 to 8 servings)

> 2 lbs. cooked lobster meat chopped
> 2 cups thin cream sauce
> ½ tsp. garlic salt
> dash of Tabasco sauce
> 2 tsp. lemon juice
> breadcrumbs for top
> 2 tbs. butter

Add lobster meat and seasonings to hot cream sauce. Spoon mixture into a well-buttered casserole. Top with fine dry breadcrumbs. Drizzle melted butter over top. Brown in oven (375°).

14. *Scalloped Oysters*   (6 servings)

> 1 pt. oysters drained (reserve liquid)
> 2 cups freshly crushed cracker crumbs
> ½ cup butter melted
> ¼ tsp. Worcestershire sauce
> ½ tsp. salt
> ⅛ tsp. pepper
> 1 cup liquid (oyster liquor and milk)
> paprika (for top)

Combine crumbs, salt, pepper, and butter. Sprinkle ⅓ of mixture in a buttered casserole, and cover with a layer of oysters. Repeat layers. Add Worcestershire sauce to liquid, and pour over dish. Sprinkle remaining crumbs over top. Garnish with paprika. Bake in a 350° oven 30 min., or until nicely browned.

15. *Oyster Loaf*

> 1 loaf French bread
> 3 tbs. butter softened
> 2 doz. oysters (reserve liquid for basting)
> ½ cup cream
> 1 tbs. chopped celery
> 1 tbs. minced fresh parsley
> dash of Tabasco sauce
> salt and pepper

Cut off top crust of bread in one piece. Remove soft part of bread and spread lightly with softened butter; toast. Set hollowed-out loaf aside. Fry 2 doz. oysters in butter (additional) by your favorite recipe. When oysters have been turned and browned on second side, remove, and add to pan drippings the cream, celery, parsley, and other seasonings; mix well. Then stir in about ⅓ of the toasted bread (crumble it well); reserve surplus crumbs for other use. Stir fried oysters into mixture, and spoon mixture into hollowed-out loaf. Top with the crust. Place on a sheet of aluminum foil, crinkling foil to fit loosely as a nest for the bread loaf. Bake 20 min. in a 375° oven, and baste with any reserved oyster liquid. To serve, place loaf and its foil nest on a large serving platter. At the table, slice and serve.

10. Foreign Intrigue

NEW YORK CITY'S many fine restaurants, specializing in native dishes of very nearly every country in the world, offer an abundance of riches for selection of note in this chapter. The limitation of thirteen was dictated by space. The variety—including steamship, airline, restaurant and hotel—upholds the native cuisine of each land in the finest tradition of gourmet dining.

FRENCH

The Americana

The New York City **Americana**—a name synonymous with fabulous design, food, and service—has received wide acclaim from celebrities and the general public. The Imperial Ballroom, decorated in exquisite taste, is one of many rooms available for social functions. The acknowledged genius of Claude C. Philippe, managing director, in all details of Haute cuisine, provides the four-star guarantee of superlative dining.

1. *Salmon Layka*
   Carefully poach a whole 15 lb. salmon (with head and tail on) in a court bouillon. Remove from fire after cooking for 40 min. and allow to cool. Cover with a white chaud-froid and then place a border of truffle design around edge of salmon. Carefully cut a large oval out of center of chaud-froided salmon so that the pink

The Americana's lavish buffet display to mark the opening of the New York hotel. Restaurant executive staff appear at left.

salmon meat is exposed. Now make a small medallion of chaud-froid and place in center of salmon making sure some of the pink meat is exposed. Decorate with truffle design. Trim salmon tail and fins and glaze with a clear fish aspic. Place on a tray and garnish with parsley and lemon baskets and cucumber rosettes.

2. *Lobster Parisienne*
Empty the shells of two 6 lb. lobsters that have been cooked in a court bouillon. Attach to a triangular lobster stand. Carefully slice the meat from the lobster tail on a bias and rearrange on the backside of the lobster. Between each slice, place a truffle design. With an egg paste, tube out a border around slices of meat. Glaze with a clear aspic. Garnish with lemon baskets, cubes of lobster meat, and parsley sprigs.

3. *Turkey Marcella*
Roast an 18 lb. turkey, allow to cool, and cover with a brown chaud-froid. Make a medallion of white chaud-froid and place on turkey. Place a border of truffle design around medallion and trim the medallion with egg paste. Out of truffle, green pepper, and egg white of boiled egg, make a mosaic design. Glaze with a clear aspic. Place turkey on a silver platter and arrange turkey slices. Garnish with deviled eggs and aspic croutons.

CHINESE
House of Chan

The **House of Chan** has been a gourmet rendezvous since 1938. Recently, it was completely redecorated in the contemplative spirit of an ancient Chinese garden. The decorations and the food are equally tasteful and authentic, both harking back to the most spiritually rewarding of all Chinese dynasties.

Far removed from the usual chop suey provender, the ten-page menu of the **House of Chan** offers many savory splendors. The following are recipes for five of their most treasured hors d'oeuvres.

1. *Barbecued Spareribs* (4 servings)

>   1 clove garlic mashed
>   ½ cup soy sauce
>   ½ cup sugar
>   1 tsp. salt
>   ¼ tsp. pepper
>   2½ or 3 lb. piece young spareribs (whole piece)
>   1 tbs. grated orange peel

Mix garlic, soy sauce, sugar, salt, pepper, and orange peel. Trim fat from spareribs; do not chop or break; use the piece whole. Place meat in a shallow pan, pour the garlic sauce over it, and spread over meat. Let stand in the refrigerator ½ to 1 hr. Turn the meat 2 or 3 times in that time, spreading the sauce over it thoroughly each time.

To barbecue in the broiler, place the meat curved side down on a rack in a baking pan. Preheat the broiler 15 min.; place the rib pan 6 to 8 in. from med. flame for about 20 min. When the meat is crusty and done on one side, turn it and continue the cooking until the other side is browned. Total cooking time is 40 to 50 min., depending on how hot the broiler is.

2. *Shrimp Puff*

>   ½ lb. med. shrimps shelled and deveined
>   1 sm. loaf of unsliced Italian bread
>   ½ tsp. salt
>   ⅛ tsp. pepper

Pound the shrimps one by one with a flat object. Place it on board and have a rolling pin roll it over into a dough. Add salt and pepper to season it according to taste. Put the dough into a mixing bowl and lift it up in mid-air and drop it with force to the bowl. Repeat this pounding 6 times.

Slice the bread to ¼ in. slices. Spread ½ in. of the dough on the bread and cover it with another slice of bread-like sandwich. Cut shape to your own liking. Deep fry it until the bread becomes brown toast.

The House of Chan exhibits this Chinese delicacy on a typical and meticulous table setting.

3. *Beef Sate*   (4 servings)

    ¾ lb. tenderloin cut in 1 in. squares
    1 tsp. soy sauce
    ⅛ tsp. juice of fresh ginger root (may be obtained from Chinatown)
    2 tsp. sherry wine
    2 tsp. sugar
    1 can cracker meal
    4 bamboo sticks

Mix the meat, soy sauce, ginger juice, sherry wine, and sugar and marinate for 1 hr. Then roll it over the cracker meal. Hold a bamboo stick and pierce through the center of the meat—have 3 squares on each stick. Deep fry the steak for 5 min.

4. *Dem Sem*   (6 dem sems)

    ¾ lb. ground pork tenderloin
    6 pieces finely chopped water chestnuts
    1 tsp. glutamate or Accent
    1 tsp. soy sauce
    ¼ tsp. pepper
    ½ tsp. salt
    ½ tsp. sugar
    6 pieces Won Ton Skin (a kind of readymade pastry shell which may be obtained from Chinatown)

In the center of each Won Ton Skin, place 1 tbs. of filling. Fold each square into a triangular shape; press edges together, but leave point of triangle open a little. Steam in high flame for 15 min.

5. *Treasure Roll*   (4 rolls)

Filling:

    3 lbs. celery cabbage in fine slices
    1 lb. bamboo shoots in fine slices
    10 pieces water chestnuts in fine slices

A twenty-one gun salute to the "21" Club—that haven of warm hospitality to the regular, remains the Mt. Everest of restaurants to the initiated.

1 oz. dry Chinese mushrooms (soak them in warm water for
   1 hr. before cutting in fine slices)

3 pieces scallions minced (green and white)

½ lb. lobster meat diced

1 tsp. salt

½ tsp. pepper

2 tbs. soy sauce

1 piece coal fat cut into 4 squares

1 can cracker meal

3 eggs beaten

Place celery cabbage and bamboo shoots in about ½ cup boiling water; cover and cook till steaming. Drain at once, roll in clean towel; press well to remove as much moisture as possible. Mix the above ingredients except coal fat, cracker meal, and eggs, and have it ready for the filling of the Treasure Roll.

To roll, lay one piece of coal fat on the table. Place 3 or 4 table-spoons of filling on each square. Spread the filling lengthwise, then fold the pastry edge which is along the length of the filling over the filling; then fold one end over this, then the other end, and last the remaining side. Fold this over the roll and press lightly together. Paste the roll over with beaten eggs and roll it over with cracker meal.

Steam the roll for 20 min. Wait until it is completely cold, then deep fry for 10 min. until golden brown all around.

INTERNATIONAL

"21" Club

To attempt to limit the matchless cuisine of **"21" Club** to the background of one nationality is impossible. This is a restaurant with an international reputation and a special aura of affectionate approval that stretches around the world. As in the preparation of all fine foods, the French master's touch is evident, but as Executive Chef Louis Ploneis says in his usual amiable fashion, "We give the guests what they ask for." This interest in pleasing the guest and making him feel a warmth and welcome that lifts him immediately to heights of unsurpassed importance is the spirit that induces the joy of dining at "**21**."

1. *Stuffed Clams "21"*
   Open 4 doz. Little Neck Clams (save 48 half-shells). Chop finely and bring to boil in own juice.

   In separate pan, simmer in butter 2 tbs. of chopped shallots, 2 cloves of garlic, and 1 tsp. of oregano. Strain clam juice into this mixture and reduce to about ⅔. Thicken with a little flour and butter. Add 2 tbs. of chives. Mix clams in the thick sauce and add a few drops of Worcestershire sauce. Put clam mixture in half-shells. Sprinkle with breadcrumbs and Parmesan cheese. Brown under broiler and serve.

2. *Chicken Bits*
   Remove all meat from two 2½ lb. raw chickens. Cut into bit slices. Sprinkle with salt and pepper. Sauté in very hot butter until almost cooked. Sprinkle with a little sweet basil. Turn once and remove from fire. Let it cool. Wrap each piece with bacon and secure with a toothpick. Fry in deep hot fat or cook in oven until bacon is crispy.

3. *Beef Bordelaise*
   Five lbs. of tenderloin of beef cut in pieces about the size of a half-dollar, but slightly thicker. Sauté in butter or vegetable oil until rare. Cook half-cup of finely chopped shallots. Add 1 qt. of Bordeaux red wine. Reduce to about ½ and add 1 gal. of brown gravy, reducing again to ⅔. Add beef and simmer (do not boil). Decorate with about 20 slices of marrow. Sprinkle with chopped parsley and serve.

4. *Goujonnettes of Sole*
   Three lbs. of lemon sole cut in pieces about the thickness of a pencil and 2 in. long. Sprinkle with salt and pepper and roll in palm of hand. Bread by first dipping in flour, then 2 beaten eggs, and then in white breadcrumbs. Fry in deep hot fat, shortening, or vegetable oil. Serve hot with tartare and cocktail sauce.

5. *Caviar Blinis*
Make small buckwheat pancakes (about 2½ in. across). Cover with caviar and top with sour cream. Serve with an extra blini plain.

DUTCH

KLM Royal Dutch Airlines

KLM Royal Dutch Airlines, flying to 104 cities in 68 countries throughout the world, takes special pride in the preparation and presentation of its food. **KLM** chefs are trained on the Continent. Their entrees and canapés evoke praise from even the most critical of gourmets. Individual requests, such as Kosher meals, special diet foods, and vegetarian meals, are handled with ease by the airline. The following are some Dutch delicacies that delight **KLM** passengers.

1. *Smoked Eel—Anguille Fumee*
Remove eel skin and cut lengthwise starting by the tail over the main bone into two fillets. Cut the fillets in pieces about 1 in. long.

2. *Aspic for Pâté De Foie Gras* (for 24 slices)

    1 qt. rich meat stock
    1 oz. granulated gelatine

When the stock that is to be used has been properly seasoned and the gelatine has been added, the following method is used to clarify it if necessary. Beat 2 egg whites until foamy. Add ½ tsp. salt and 1 tsp. cooking brandy. Stir this mixture into the stock and heat to the boiling point. Remove from the fire and pour the stock through a double cheesecloth. If the jelly is pale, add a little sugar coloring.

KLM Royal Dutch Airlines' flight kitchen at Idlewild Airport is where Catering Manager Jan de Hann and Chef Cornelis Stekelenburg supervise the preparation of hors d'oeuvres for first-class passengers.

To glaze the slices of goose liver, cut the goose liver in slices ½ in. thick, put the slices on a wire rack and store in refrigerator. Put some liquid jelly in a metal bowl and place it in the pan with some water and cracked ice. Stir the jelly to prevent setting. The jelly must hang and be put quickly over the slices of goose liver; store again in refrigerator for 20 min. To line a platter or tray, put enough liquid jelly to cover the bottom and store in refrigerator until the jelly is firm; decorate the jelly layer with little figures cut from the white end of a hard boiled egg, black olives, or make little flowers from a peeled tomato and stringbeans. Cover the tray with a second layer of jelly and store in refrigerator. The tray is now ready to put the goose liver on it and to be garnished with some watercress.

3. *Darne De Saumon Froid*

> cut off cold salmon for 24 servings
> 12 each 1 lb. slices of fresh salmon
> white wine
> water
> ½ oz. salt
> ½ tsp. white peppercorns
> 1 bouquet garni
> ½ each sliced onion
> 1 each sliced carrot

In a pan large enough to cook the salmon, pour equal amounts of water and white wine—enough to cover the fish which will be put in later. Add salt, pepper, bouquet garni, sliced onion, and carrot. Cover the pan and simmer for ½ hr. Put in the salmon and let it simmer until cooked—never let it boil. Let the salmon cool in the "court bouillon". Drain thoroughly; remove the skin and bones carefully and cut in half. Decorate with sprig of parsley and thin slices of lemon. Place in long platter or tray with some lettuce. Encircle the salmon with stuffed eggs and 24 small pieces of smoked eel 1 in. long. Serve with bowl of mayonnaise.

*The Waldorf-Astoria's Bull and Bear Restaurant present dishes true
to traditional British cuisine. At left is Executive Chef Eugene
Scanlan; at right, Nicholas Sepcich, chef in charge of the kitchen.*

ENGLISH
The Waldorf Astoria's Bull and Bear

The traditional fame of old English pubs was enhanced both in
style and dignity when the world-famous **Waldorf Astoria** opened
the **Bull and Bear** restaurant as one of several dining rooms of unusual distinction. Hearty British fare dominates the menu. Chef
Scanlan's deepest affection for fine food is centered here where
the solid virtue of sturdy meals complements the oak furniture and
masculine prints in the background.

1. *Veal and Ham Pie*

Crust

> 1½ cups sifted flour
> ½ tsp. salt
> ⅓ cup shortening
> 3 tbs. cold water or more

Filling

> 1 lb. veal loin cut in 1 in. dices
> ½ lb. lean, raw, smoked ham cut in 1 in. squares
> 2 hard cooked eggs coarsely chopped
> 1 tsp. salt
> 2 tsp. chopped parsley
> ½ lemon rind grated
> ⅛ tbs. well-seasoned meat stock

Sift dry ingredients together. Cut in shortening. Add water to make stiff paste and mix lightly. Allow to rest a few minutes. Roll out on a well floured board. To make filling, arrange veal and bacon or ham in layers in well-greased casserole with eggs, lemon rind, and parsley between. Add seasoning and the stock. Cover with pastry; brush with butter. Bake for 30 min. in a hot oven (400°). Reduce heat to moderate oven (350°) and continue to bake for 1 hr. If crust browns too much, cover with brown paper.

2. *Steak and Kidney Pie*   (5 servings)

> 2 beef kidneys
> 1 lb. round steak
> 1½ tbs. fat
> ½ tsp. sugar
> 1 tbs. flour
> ½ cup sliced onions
> 3 cups stock (or 3 cups water with 1 tbs. beef extract)
> ⅛ tsp. pepper
> 3 tsp. salt

Luchow's genial host and owner, Jan Mitchell, makes daily detailed checks of traditional menu items.

pie crust or rough puff paste for topping
1 egg white slightly beaten

Soak kidneys in salt water for 30 min. Cut steak and kidneys in 1 in. cubes. Melt fat in saucepan; add sugar and beat until sugar is caramelized. Add pieces of meat and sauté until brown on all sides. Blend in flour, add remaining ingredients, and simmer for 1½ hrs. or until meat is tender. Cool slightly; place meat and onions in baking dish; add liquid to almost cover, saving the rest for gravy. Cover the dish with pastry. Make a small hole in center of the crust and decorate with leaves cut from pastry. Brush with egg white and bake in a hot (425° F.) oven for 25 to 30 min. or until brown. Serve hot with remaining gravy. Potatoes and a root vegetable or green peas are often served with the pie.

3. *Buckingham Eggs*

6 slices white toast
1½ tbs. anchovy paste
2 tbs. butter
6 eggs
½ tsp. salt
⅛ tsp. pepper
1½ tsp. butter
3 tbs. grated cheese

Butter toast and spread with anchovy paste. Beat eggs, add seasoning, and scramble in butter. (Be sure to leave eggs underdone.) Mound on toast and sprinkle with cheese. Place in hot oven (450° F.) for 4 to 5 min., or until cheese melts. Serve at once.

GERMAN

Lüchow's

Eighty years of tradition and warm nostalgia for the leisure of princely dining make **Lüchow's** famous restaurant a landmark of historic and sentimental delight. Since Jan Mitchell bought **Lü-chow's** twelve years ago, he has emphasized the old-world charm of fine food, excellent service, and warm welcome to his guests. Many special festivals mark the seasons here, but the most wonderful of all is the famous Christmas Tree. If Virginia had gone to **Lüchow's** at Christmas time, she would never have written to the New York *Sun* her plaintive letter. It is obvious that as long as Lüchow's Christmas Tree stands, there must be a Santa Claus.

1. *Herring Salat*   (6 servings)

> 4 salt herrings
> 6 boiled potatoes
> 3 apples
> 4 sour dill pickles
> 2 cooked beets
> boiled veal knuckle
> 1 green pepper
> ½ onion
> dash of black pepper
> 1 tsp. sugar
> ½ tsp. dry mustard
> ½ cup olive oil
> ½ cup wine vinegar
> 1 cup stock or bouillon
> 6 fresh lettuce leaves
> 3 tbs. capers
> 3 hard cooked eggs

Rinse herrings, drain, cover with cold water and let soak overnight. Drain, remove skin, cut fillets from bones. Dice filets fine. Peel and dice potatoes; peel, core, and dice apples; dice pickles, beets, meat, green pepper, and onion. Combine all with fish in a shallow dish. Sprinkle with onion, pepper, sugar, and mustard. Pour oil, vinegar, and stock over all. Cover and let chill in refrigerator. Serve on crisp lettuce garnished with capers and hard cooked egg quarters or slices.

2. *Speck Salat* (Hot Potato Salad with Bacon)   (2 to 4 servings)

    1 lb. (3 med.) potatoes
    6 slices bacon diced
    ½ cup vinegar
    ½ cup stock or bouillon
    1 tsp. salt
    ¼ tsp. pepper
    1 tsp. sugar
    1 egg yolk beaten

Scrub potatoes; rinse. Boil in jackets; let cool. Peel and cut in ¼ in. slices. Cook bacon in hot pan until crisp. Add onion; stir and cook until transparent. Add vinegar, stock or bouillon, and seasonings. Stir; let come to a boil. Stir in egg; remove from heat and pour over potatoes.

3. *Schlemmerschnitte*   (4 servings)

    2 lbs. filet of beef
    4 slices freshly buttered toast
    4 tbs. fresh black caviar
    1½ tbs. chopped onion

Remove all fat from beef. Grind meat fine. Arrange on toast; garnish with caviar; serve with chopped onions on a side dish.

HUNGARIAN

The Sherry Netherland

For a hotel such as **The Sherry Netherland,** which excels in the finest cuisine in the Continental manner, to be designated as "Hungarian" may pose a question. However, the inspired touch of Paul Kovi, director of catering and sales, has added savory Hungarian canapés and hors d'oeuvres to the menu at the cocktail hour in La Petite, the charmingly intimate dining room overlooking Central Park. Here gather the sophisticated crowds, whose taste and inclination tend to the exotic. Background, service and, above all, the

At the Sherry Netherland's La Petite, meticulous care is given to the arrangement of the hors d'oeuvres tray.

unusual and delicious appetizers meet and surpass the demands of the cocktail-hour capacity crowds.

HUNGARIAN CANAPÉS AND HORS D'OEUVRES

The cuisine in Hungarian hotels is, and always was, under the influence of French cuisine. Therefore, there will be in most of the Hungarian presentations of hors d'oeuvres some underlying traits of French culinary art. However, there are a few combinations which are based on traditional Hungarian cooking.

1. *Cold Canapés*

One of the favorite cheese presentations for cold canapés is the so-called Korozott cheese, which is a cheese spread based on ⅓ cream cheese, ⅓ mountain goat cheese, and ⅓ butter spiced with paprika, caraway seed, mustard, salt, pepper, chopped chives and fresh dill, slightly fermented with a touch of beer. This finely colored cheese spread is widely used in several combinations. It can be combined with the very unique Hungarian sausage called *csabai kolbasz* and served on a small cut of homey black bread, or with the famous Hungarian Hertz salami shaped in a cornet decorated with watercress. Very often the cheese spread is stuffed tightly into yellow, green, and red waxed peppers put in the refrigerator for half a day and, before serving, cut into attractive rings and served on toast.

One of the truly delicate cold canapés is the finger toast of cold pickled calves brains with light cold Bearnaise sauce, flavored with fresh dill. Also, finger toasts of smoked carp flavored with paprika.

A very colorful presentation in the traditional Hungarian national colors of red, white, and green is red radishes scooped out and stuffed with white mountain goat cheese, which is flavored with fresh dill and decorated with fresh watercress leaves.

2. *Hot Hors D'Oeuvres*

Breaded and fried mushroom caps flavored with mayonnaise and fresh chopped dill. Fried calves' brains balls on skewers. Chest-

*San Marino host, "Tony," supervises the fine Northern Italian spe-
cialties that have made this restaurant a gourmet's paradise.*

nuts wrapped in bacon. Ramekins stuffed with calves' brains and eggs. Recipe for this is as follows: Finely chopped smoked bacon, braised to light brown with finely chopped onions. Then allow to simmer under cover for an additional 5 min. Cook 1 average-size calf's brain in water, lightly salted, and flavored with lemon. When done, take out, remove skin, dice finely, and mix in chopped parsley, salt, pepper, and 2 eggs. Cook with onions on high heat for 5 min. Fold into ramekins. Cover lightly with Parmesan cheese, put in oven for additional 5 min., and serve.

3. *Chicken Livers in Paprika Sauce*
Braise finely chopped onions to golden brown. Add paprika, chicken livers, marjoram, and pepper. Reduce with small quantity of red wine. Serve with rice from chafing dishes.

Very well known are the Hungarian bite-size stuffed cabbages served all over the world, especially in New York City. An additional unusual chafing dish item is the:

4. *Sour Beef Lung*
Cook the lung in water with whole onions, bay leaves, whole pepper kernels, a touch of sugar, vinegar, and salt until done. For the sauce, make a light roux; add the liquid from the lung to roux; flavor with salt and mustard. Take out lung from its original "soup" and slice into 1 in. cuts. Simmer it in sauce for 15 min. Add lemon to taste. Serve with rice.

ITALIAN

The San Marino

Nestling a few steps below street level, **The San Marino** offers Northern Italian dishes done with the master touch of Tony Grignoni. Inpeccable service in a room of quiet distinction adds to an unforgettable experience in fine dining.

1. *Caponatina À La San Marino*   (4 servings)

Each med. size eggplant should yield about 12 ¼ in. thick slices—
enough for 4 portions. The diameter of eggplants vary. However,
the size of both the onion and tomato should approximate the
diameter of the eggplant. This will give uniformity, make preparation easier, and make final presentation more appealing.

> 1 med. size eggplant sliced in ¼ in. thick slices with skin on
>   (should make 12 slices)
> 2 large beefsteak tomatoes sliced in ¼ in. thick slices (should
>   make 8 slices)
> 1 lg. onion cut in ⅛ in. thick slices (should make 8 slices)
> ½ cup savory tomato sauce
> 12 black olives pitted and sliced
> 4 tsp. capers
> 4 cloves garlic sliced paper thin
> 4 tbs. olive oil
> 4 tbs. wine vinegar
> salt and pepper to taste

(1) Soak sliced eggplant in salted cold water for about 5 min. Drain
thoroughly and arrange in baking pan.

(2) Place 1 tbs. of sauce in the baking dish and a slice of eggplant
over it. Follow with a slice of tomato and, on top of that, a slice
of onion. In between add a dash of the tomato sauce, capers and
garlic, and black olives. Repeat this procedure, topping it with a
third slice of eggplant. The formed "sandwich" should be like
this: eggplant, tomato, onion, eggplant, tomato, onion, eggplant.
This stack comprises 1 portion.

(3) Repeat in line 3 more times to form 4 "stacks."

(4) Top each stack with the remaining tomato sauce. Sprinkle
lightly with olive oil and vinegar.

(5) Cover the pan with aluminum foil and bake in a 325 to 350°
oven for about 1 hr. Remove and chill thoroughly. Serve cold.

2. *Mussels À La San Marino*   (4 portions)

> 2 lbs. mussels (in shells)

2 tbs. olive oil
2 cloves garlic
1½ cups white wine (dry)
2 tbs. finely chopped scallions
2 tbs. finely chopped celery
1 tbs. finely chopped parsley
breadcrumbs

(1) Scrub mussels thoroughly under clear cold running water, taking care to remove all "whiskers" for a clean shell.
(2) Brown garlic in olive oil, add the mussels, scallions, celery, parsley, and white wine, and simmer until mussels open easily and liquid is reduced to half.
(3) Remove top shell of mussel and discard. Arrange mussel, which is in lower shell, on a pan and sprinkle lightly with breadcrumbs.
(4) Baste with the liquid in which the mussels were cooked, and brown under a broiler. Serve hot with a lemon wedge.

3. *Cappelletti*   (4 servings)

Noodle

1½ cups strong flour
4 egg yolks
water

(1) On a pastry board, make a well in the flour, and add the egg yolks. Slowly mix the flour and eggs, working the mixture well with hands for about 20 min. Add water, if necessary, to insure a dough of proper consistency.
(2) Roll dough out on a well-floured board with a rolling pin until it is very thin.
(3) With a 2 or 3 in. cookie cutter, cut circles from the dough.
(4) Place about 1 tsp. full of the filling in the center of each round of dough.
(5) Fold over the dough, turnover fashion, and seal the edges.
(6) Boil the cappelletti in salted boiling water, or chicken broth, for 20 min., or until tender.

The Miyako's specialty, sukiyaki, is prepared before the critical eyes of its manager, Miss Aya. Tempura and Japanese salad are placed in perfect symmetry before her.

(7) Drain well and place in a pan with melted clarified butter. Serve hot with fresh grated Parmesan cheese.

Stuffing

> 3 slices of crisp cooked bacon finely chopped
> ¼ lb. boiled chicken (white meat finely chopped)
> 2 ozs. roast pork finely chopped
> 1 whole egg
> 2 tsp. Parmesan cheese (grated)
> salt and pepper and a pinch of nutmeg

Mix all ingredients together until well blended.

JAPANESE

Miyako Restaurant

The gentle courtesy that greets the guest at the **Miyako Restaurant** sets the theme for a typical lunch or dinner with the quiet dignity of Japanese service where native waiters move with characteristic ease and grace. Serene Japanese prints give added distinction to the room. Each table is set with the exact neatness of a blueprint, dominated by the impressive equipment for the preparation of the suki-yaki cooked at the table while the guest's eyes and nose are enchanted by the colors and aromas of the ingredients.

1. *Shrimp Tempura*

Batter

> 1 cup flour
> 1 egg
> 1 cup water
> pinch of salt
> ¼ tsp. sugar
> (this quantity of batter can be easily enlarged, merely by doubling all the quantities)

Blend all ingredients together to produce a somewhat lumpy batter.

Shrimp

Dip the raw, peeled, and deveined shrimp into the batter and deep fry in vegetable oil which is at 400° until a rich golden color is achieved. (It should be noted, that in addition to shrimp, string beans, asparagus tips, carrot pieces, squash, celery tips, eggplant, cauliflower, sweet peppers, and watercress can be prepared using this batter, merely by dipping the item into the batter and deep frying it as the shrimp. All items prepared in this manner should first be fried from the raw stage.)

Sauce

> 3 parts soup stock (Dashi—see below)
> 1 part merin (sweet cooking sake)
> 1 part soy sauce
> grated white radish
> grated ginger (fresh)

Blend all ingredients together except radish and ginger. Bring to a boil. Just before serving, add the white radish and grated ginger.

Dashi (Stock)

> ½ cup dried Bonito
> 1 sq. in. tangle of seaweed
> 5 cups water
> ¼ teaspoon Accent

Place seaweed in water and bring to a boil. Remove seaweed. Add Bonito and again bring to a boil. Remove from heat. Allow Bonito to sink to the bottom. Drain off clear liquid from the top. Add Accent. This is the Dashi or stock.

2. *Sukiyaki* (Beef)   (5 portions)

   1 lb. rib roast cut in paper thin slices
   6 ozs. spinach
   6 ozs. scallions
   6 ozs. Chinese cabbage
   2 pieces bean curd
   12 mushrooms
   Shiratoki (canned)
   5 eggs (1 per portion)
   2 cups sukiyaki sauce (see below)

Place sukiyaki sauce in a pan and let it come to a boil. Add all the rest of the ingredients, starting with the meat and arranging them in layers except for the eggs. Cover and allow to cook until the vegetables are cooked and tender. The beaten eggs are then added if desired. Rice may be served if desired also.

3. *Sukiyaki Sauce*

   1⅓ cups Dashi
   ¾ cups soy sauce
   ¼ cup sugar
   4 tsp. merin

Bring all ingredients to a boil, blending well.

4. *Salad Dressing*

   1 cup vinegar (white distilled)
   ⅓ cup water
   1 tsp. salt
   2 tsp. sake
   pinch aji

Blend all ingredients together thoroughly and keep refrigerated until ready to use.

Justine Caterers offers this varied assortment of delicious kosher hors d'oeuvres to set the stage for traditional dining.

KOSHER

Justine Catering Company

The **Justine Catering Company** is one of many houses specializing in kosher foods for various social affairs with religious backgrounds. Strict dietary laws are observed in the traditional manner. Creative imagination in artistic displays and table arrangements as well as highly personalized service give **Justine** that extra special something for events of catered memory.

1. *Potato Pancakes*   (36 pancakes)

> 3 lbs. raw peeled potatoes
> 2 med. onions
> 3 eggs
> 1 tbs. salt (pepper to taste)
> ½ tsp. baking powder
> 1 cup flour
> pinch nutmeg

Grate or grind potatoes. Remove all liquid. Add grated onions and eggs. Mix well; sift flour and all dry ingredients. Add to above.

(1) Heat oil or shortening in fry pan.
(2) Drop heaping tablespoons of potato mixture in hot oil.
(3) Fry to a golden brown on both sides.
(4) Serve with applesauce.

2. *Kreplach*

Filling

> 3 cups cooked chicken meat
> 1 med. onion sautéed golden
> 2 hard boiled eggs
> salt and pepper to taste

Grind all above ingredients very fine. Add salt and pepper.

Noodle Dough

    3 eggs
    ¼ tsp. salt
    ¼ cup water
    all-purpose flour—to make a soft dough

Beat eggs. Add salt and water. Stir in enough flour to make a soft
dough. Knead for 3 or 4 min. on floured board. Roll out in thin
sheet and cut in 2 in. squares.

Put 1 tbs. of filling on each square. Fold over to form triangle.
Press edges of dough together to seal in the filling. Cook in boiling salted water for 15 min. Remove from water and cool.

To serve, heat in fry pan with sautéed onions. Sprinkle with
paprika.

3. *Pastrami Chicken Livers*   (12 servings)

    12 chicken livers
    12 slices pastrami
    6 water chestnuts cut in halves

(1) Broil chicken livers.
(2) Place ½ slice water chestnut on liver.
(3) Wrap with slice pastrami.
(4) Secure with toothpick.
(5) Heat in moderate oven 10 min.
(6) Serve hot.

4. *Stuffed Mushrooms*   (24 mushrooms)

    24 med. mushrooms
    1 lb. chuck chopped
    1 sm. onion fine diced and sautéed
    1 egg
    2 slices challah (or bread)
    ½ cup chicken stock
    salt and pepper to taste

(1) Remove stems from mushrooms.

(2) Wash mushrooms; then drain.

(3) Soak challah in chicken stock.

(4) Squeeze out excess liquid.

(5) Mix chopped meat, onion, egg, and challah.

(6) Add salt and pepper to taste.

(7) Stuff meat mixture into mushroom caps.

(8) Bake on greased sheet pan in a moderate oven for 15 min. or until meat is done.

5. *Caviar Blintzes* (24 blintzes)

4 to 8 in. blintzes (cut 6 wedges to each)

On each wedge of blintz dough, put one teaspoon black caviar. Then sprinkle with chopped chives and parsley and add a touch of lemon juice. Fold and roll to shape. Heat in a slow oven until warm.

LATIN AMERICAN
La Fonda Del Sol

The hot-blooded romantic excitement of Latin America has been captured at **La Fonda Del Sol** with such exciting impact that the visitor is left breathless with wonder and delight. Service by a well-trained staff in colorful uniforms includes graphic explanation of the imaginative menu. Chef John Santi has devised a widely varied adventure in food to tempt the most jaded appetite, from the delicious assortment of appetizers on through the unique desserts. **La Fonda** presents dramatic dining.

1. *Camarones En Salsa Verde* (Shrimp in Mexican Green Sauce)

1 lb. tomatillos (Mexican green tomatoes)

1 tsp. cilantro chopped

2 cloves garlic

2 lg. green peppers (seeds removed)

2 sm. hot green peppers

La Fonda Del Sol's chef, John Santi, checks each item on an elaborate table of delicious appetizers gleaned from many Latin American countries.

½ bunch parsley stems
1 cup vinegar

Mix all ingredients together in a saucepan and bring to a boil. Let simmer until peppers and tomatoes are soft. If more liquid is necessary, add a little more water. When cooked, remove from fire and pass through food choppers; let cool. Then mix with equal amount of mayonnaise; season and mix well. Add shrimps that have been boiled, shelled and deveined. Serve cold. (The green Mexican tomato has a thin onion-like covering which must be removed before cooking.)

2. *Guacamole* (Avocado Salad)

    6 each ripe avocados
    3 each diced small tomatoes
    ½ each aji pepper
    ½ tsp. chopped fresh coriander (cilantro)
    2 each finely diced red onions
    juice of 3 lemons
    salt to taste

Peel avocados. Guacamole should be part puree, but with some small pieces of avocado visible. Be sure not to overmash the avocado. Cube tomato, chop the cilantro very fine, and dice red onions fine. Add all these ingredients to the avocado and mix slightly. Then add lemon juice and chopped aji pepper, according to taste. Season with salt and serve cold.

3. *Anticuchos Mixtos* (Grilled Peruvian Tidbits on Skewers)
Anticuchos are Peruvian appetizers made from beef, veal heart, and chicken liver. One portion of anticuchos should contain about 10 skewers of meat, 4 beef, 4 veal hearts, and 2 chicken livers.

The skewers are placed in a marination (see No. 4 below) for 2 hrs. before cooking. The oil in the marination is the only oil needed for cooking of the anticuchos. The anticuchos can be cooked over charcoal or on a hot grill. Each piece of meat on the skewer should be about ½ oz. in weight; therefore, they must be cooked quickly and served at once. Dice the beef into squares about ½ oz. each. Place 4 pieces on skewer, 5 in. long, about 1 in. apart. The same for veal hearts and chicken livers. The veal should be free from all veins and muscles and the chicken liver completely clean.

4. *Marination*

> ¼ oz. crushed aji pepper
> juice from ½ lime
> juice from 1 lemon
> 1 oz. of oil
> 1 oz. of water
> pinch of garlic
> half of bay leaf
> salt to taste

After the anticuchos have marinated 2 hrs., they are cooked on a hot fire. Served with anticucho sauce and a fresh green salad.

5. *Salsa De Anticucho*   (1 qt. approx.)

> 1½ qts. chicken stock
> 7 ozs. chili powder
> ½ cup tomato puree
> 1 med. onion chopped
> 2 cloves garlic chopped
> ½ cup oil
> ½ cup flour

Sauté onions and garlic in oil. Add flour, hot chicken stock, and tomato puree. Dissolve chili powder in as much water as needed and pour into saucepan in which chicken stock, onion, etc., are boiling. Reduce the heat and simmer about 30 min. Strain and season to taste. Add as much Salsa Picante or Tabasco as taste requires to finish anticucho sauce.

6. *Masa De Empanada* (Empanada Dough) (15 to 18 empanadas)

>   4 ozs. lard
>   11 ozs. flour
>   1 oz. oil
>   3 eggs (1 egg for wash)
>   4 ozs. water (approx.)

Whip lard until fluffy. Add flour; mix. Add oil and eggs; mix well. Then add water a little at a time until dough has smooth consistency. Mix dough well until it does not stick to fingers. Remove from mixing bowl and store in refrigerator for 1 hr. before using. After 1 hr., roll dough out on floured table. Empanada dough should be thinner than a dime. Use an empty 1 lb. coffee can to cut out the empanadas. Remove all extra dough which is cut away from each circle. Whip up one egg well, wash each circle, and place on it ¾ oz. filling. Fold over to form half-moon shape; twist ends close by overlap dough, such as on pie shell. Put points down—not up. Fry in deep fat about 375° until brown.

7. *Relleno De Empanada* (Empanada Filling) (for 15 empanadas)

>   ½ clove garlic chopped
>   1 med. chopped onion
>   3 ozs. pork lard
>   6 ozs. red pepper diced
>   6 ozs. green pepper diced
>   1 lb. chopped meat
>   2 ozs. raisins
>   salt
>   pepper
>   fresh aji pepper or pickled chili Jalapenos (as desired)
>   1 tbs. arrowroot
>   ¾ cup beef stock

Melt pork lard in saucepan. Add chopped onion, garlic, and diced green and red peppers. Sauté a few minutes. Add chopped beef; cook until beef turns color. Add raisins and beef broth. Boil until

*This Hawaiian Room hostess, knowing that eye appeal is essential
to good food, serves succulent appetizers at the dinner hour.*

meat and vegetables are cooked. Add as much aji or Jalapeno peppers as wished. Dilute arrowroot with a little water. Thicken filling. Correct seasoning and let cool. Use about ¾ oz. of the filling for each empanada.

POLYNESIAN

Hawaiian Room

The island paradise of Hawaii may have served as the *inspiration*, but it is the *genius* of Chef Albert Stockli that has devised dishes for the Hotel Lexington's **Hawaiian Room** to create a superlative menu. The setting is picturesque; the lovely Hawaiian hostesses add charm and glamour; and the native floor show gives the finishing touch to a dramatic background. The heart-warming sight of family groups at dinner enhances the delight of dining in the **Hawaiian Room.** From those of seven to seventy years it is impossible to tell who is having the biggest whirl.

1. Shrimp Luau   (6 large servings)

> 2 lbs. raw jumbo shrimp
> ¼ cup lemon juice (fresh, frozen, or canned)
> dash salt
> dash ginger
> 1 tsp. curry powder
> 2 cans (4 ozs. each) shredded coconut
> 3 cups sifted all-purpose flour
> 3 tsp. baking powder
> 1 tsp. salt
> few drops yellow food coloring
> 1 cup milk
> fat for deep-fat frying
> curry sauce (see No. 2 below)

Remove shell from body of shrimp, but leave shrimp tail intact. (The firm tails serve as eating handles.) Now split the back of the shrimp lengthwise with a knife. Mix the lemon juice, salt, ginger, and curry powder together. Pour over shrimp and let stand or marinate for 4 to 6 hrs. in the refrigerator.

Sprinkle coconut on a tray and bake in a 250°F oven (or very slow oven) until dry. Meanwhile, make the batter: mix flour, baking powder and salt together; stir in yellow food coloring and milk smoothly (this makes a very thick batter).

Drain shrimp from marinade, coat with additional flour, dip into thick batter and roll each shrimp in coconut. Fry in deep hot fat—fat thermometer should register 375°F—until batter is golden and coconut is deep brown in color. To serve, dip in heated curry sauce.

2. *Curry Sauce*

½ lb. leftover or boiled ham
2 med. onions
2 stalks celery
1 clove garlic
½ cup salad oil
1 cup sifted all-purpose flour
1 cup curry powder
1 can (6 ozs.) tomato paste
1 qt. chicken stock or bouillon
¼ cup lemon juice (fresh, frozen, or canned)
1 can (1 lb. 1 oz.) applesauce
¼ cup sugar
2 chicken bouillon cubes
1 tsp. salt
1 cup light cream

Work ham, onions, celery and garlic through a food grinder. Heat oil in a large saucepan, toss in ground ham mixture, and cook slowly for 10 min. Now sprinkle in flour and continue cooking over a low heat until mixture is dry looking, but not brown. Stir in curry powder (mixture is very dry here), tomato paste, chicken stock or bouillon, lemon juice, applesauce, sugar, bouillon cubes, and salt. Stir until smooth. Cover and cook slowly for about 1 hr. Mix in the cream and heat through. Pour into glass jars (makes about 2¼ qts.) and store in refrigerator. Keeps well for at least 2 weeks.

3. *Hawaiian Glazed Spareribs*   (4 servings)

> 1 cup bean sauce (see No. 4 below)
> 1 cup plum sauce (see No. 5 below)
> 2 cloves garlic
> 1½ tsp. salt
> 1 tbs. sugar
> ½ tsp. monosodium glutamate
> few drops red food coloring
> 2 tbs. salad oil
> 2 lbs. (1 rack) spareribs
> 1 can (9 ozs.) pineapple chunks

Mix bean sauce, plum sauce, crushed garlic, salt, sugar, and monosodium glutamate together in a bowl. Stir in enough red food coloring to make a nice vibrant red and beat in the oil, a drop at a time, until you have a smooth thick sauce. Put spareribs in a shallow dish and pour sauce over them. Marinate in refrigerator for several hours. (It's even better if they marinate overnight.)

Start your oven at 450°F or "hot." Remove ribs from marinade, place on a rack, and bake 10 min. Reduce heat to 325°F or "slow" and continue baking 1 hr. 20 min., or until meat is fork tender. Turn ribs occasionally and baste with marinade during roasting.

At serving time, coat ribs with remaining marinade (heated, of course) and garnish with drained pineapple chunks.

4. *Bean Sauce*

> 1 can (1 lb.) red kidney beans
> 1 tsp. soy sauce
> ½ tsp. sugar
> ½ tsp. monosodium glutamate

Work kidney beans (bean liquid too) through a food mill or sieve (or use your blender to make a bean puree). Once beans are pureed, stir in remaining ingredients. Store in glass jar to use when needed.

5. Plum Sauce   (3 cups)

>   2 cups plum or apricot preserves
>   1 cup dry English mustard
>   ⅔ cup sherry wine
>   1 tsp. cinnamon
>   1 tsp. cloves
>   1 tsp. anise
>   1 tsp. fennel

Mix all ingredients together. Spoon into a glass jar. Cover tightly and keep in refrigerator. Since this is a very hot sauce, small amounts are used in the various recipes.

6. Crepes with Crab Meat

Batter

>   ¾ cup sifted all-purpose flour
>   1 cup milk
>   2 eggs
>   shortening

Filling   (6 servings)

>   2 cans (6½ oz. size) crab meat
>   3 tbs. butter or margarine
>   4 to 5 scallions
>   ¾ cup sherry
>   2 tbs. lemon juice, fresh, frozen, or canned
>   ½ tsp. onion salt
>   1 tsp. curry powder
>   4 tsp. ginger
>   1 can (1 lb.) bean sprouts
>   mock hollandaise sauce (see separate recipe below)

Make the crepes first. Mix flour, milk, and eggs into a thin, smooth batter. Heat a small skillet (6 to 7 in. in diameter) and grease with a little shortening. Add enough batter to cover bottom of skillet, and fry until brown on both sides. Make about 15 to 18 crepes and set aside for the moment. Now make the filling. Drain crab meat, chop fine, and cook in melted butter or margarine for several minutes. Chop scallions fine and toss in with crab meat, along with sherry, lemon juice, onion salt, curry powder, ginger, and drained bean sprouts. Cook a minute or two. Spoon about 3 tbs. of the crab filling into center of each crepe and tuck in the sides to make a roll. Place in a lightly greased baking dish. Pour mock hollandaise over the top and broil in a preheated broiler until golden.

Mock Hollandaise Sauce

    ½ cup butter or margarine
    2 tbs. flour
    ¼ tsp. salt
    dash pepper
    1 cup milk or light cream
    2 egg yolks
    1 tbs. lemon juice, fresh, frozen, or canned

Melt butter or margarine in top of double boiler. Stir in flour smoothly along with salt and pepper. Add milk or cream gradually and cook over a low heat, stirring constantly, until sauce bubbles. Now place over boiling water and continue cooking 15 min. longer. Shortly before using, beat sauce into egg yolks; add lemon juice and heat over boiling water, stirring vigorously.

SWEDISH

The Swedish-American Line

Although the bill of fare on the beautiful Swedish-American liners *Gripsholm* and *Kungsholm* offer a wide variety of American and Continental delicacies, the *pièce de résistance* in dining on board is the Swedish "smorgasbord" served at eleven o'clock each evening. Here

This smorgasbord table aboard a Swedish-American liner is a veritable bower of beauty, creating a dramatic blend of taste and color.

in magnificent display are the wonderful dishes that make Scandinavian food an exciting adventure. The widest possible selection of cold meats, fish, salads, relishes, and cheeses are forerunners to the awesome casseroles of hot dishes, reflecting so unmistakenly "a bit of Sweden" afloat.

1. Swedish Herring Casserole

   6 filets of salt herring
   6 potatoes peeled and sliced thin
   4 onions sliced thin
   3 tbs. chopped dill or parsley
   1 tsp. pepper
   2 eggs
   1½ cups milk
   ¼ cup breadcrumbs
   3 tbs. butter melted

Soak the herring overnight in water. Change the water at least twice. Drain; then dry the herring. Cut into long, thin strips. In a buttered casserole, arrange layers of potatoes, herring, and onions, sprinkling each layer with pepper and dill. Beat the eggs and milk together; add to the casserole. Sprinkle with the breadcrumbs and dot with the butter. Bake in oven for 45 min. Serve hot.

2. Chicken À La Gripsholm

Cut a chicken in quarter pieces and put into a pan with 3 tbs. melted butter. Add salt and pepper, one small onion, chopped, and half a carrot, sliced.

Cover and simmer slowly without browning for about 30 min. Discard the carrot slices. Remove the chicken and keep hot. Stir ½ cup of dry white wine into the juices and reduce until almost evaporated.

Add 1 cup heavy cream, simmer for 1 min., and blend in 4 tbs. *foie gras*, creamed with 4 tbs. good cognac. Simmer for 1 to 2 min. to evaporate the alcohol. Pour the sauce over the chicken and serve very hot.

3. Crepes À La Gripsholm

> thin pancakes
> boiled lobster
> boiled or fried chicken cut into small pieces
> mushrooms
> onion finely chopped
> sherry
> white wine
> saffron
> Parmesan cheese

First make thin pancakes. Then sauté the lobster, chicken, mushrooms cut into small pieces, and the chopped onion in butter, until golden brown. Sprinkle some flour and add the sherry and white wine and let simmer until thick. Add a bit of saffron and salt to taste.

Place a good amount of the sauté on each pancake and roll together. Place in buttered baking dish. Sprinkle with Parmesan cheese and gratinate in warm oven (500°F.) about 10 to 15 min. or until nicely browned.

4. Veal Schnitzel Piquante

> thin veal cutlets
> cooked smoked ham
> thin slices of Swiss cheese
> egg
> breadcrumbs

The cutlets should be pounded out very thin. (Use two cutlets for each person.) Place a thin slice of the ham on top of a slice of veal cutlet, then two slices of Swiss cheese, and another slice of the ham. Place a second slice of veal on top and press together. Beat a couple of whole eggs with fork. Dip the meat in egg and breadcrumbs; season to taste. Pan fry very slowly in butter until golden brown.

5. Swedish Meat Balls   (6 servings)

> 2 lbs. minced meats (preferably ½ beef and ½ pork)

2 eggs
2 mashed boiled potatoes
1 onion minced and browned
1 pt. water
3 slices bread (stale, if available)
3 tsp. salt
½ tsp. pepper
butter (or other fat) for frying

Gravy

3 tbs. butter (or other fat)
¼ lb. flour
1½ to 2 pts. water (or stock)
salt and pepper to taste

Dissolve the bread in water. Brown the onion and mash the cold potatoes. Now mix all the ingredients in a large bowl and keep on working it until you have a smooth spongy mass. The potatoes tend to make the meat balls lighter. Heat the butter (or fat) in a frying pan. Shape the balls by using palm of hand. Brown evenly and well in the fat. Remove to a saucepan. Repeat until the whole mixture is used up.

Make the gravy in the same frying pan by heating butter, adding flour, and heating to a golden paste. Gradually add the water and keep stirring to avoid all lumps. For a darker gravy, add a few drops of concentrated beef juice or brown some sugar for the purpose. Most Swedish housewives add a pinch of sugar to all gravies to obtain a richer flavor. Pour gravy over the meat balls and simmer over gentle heat for ¼ hr. (Overcooking and reheating do no harm.)

Using some pork in the meat balls cuts down the quantity of fat needed in the frying process, besides adding a nice sweet flavor. For special occasions it is good to add ¼ to ½ cup of chopped mushrooms. Brown them lightly and just let them simmer with the meat balls in the gravy. Some cooks add tomatoes, paprika, and other ingredients to suit their individual palates. A cup of heavy cream, of course, always helps to enrich the gravy.

II. Sugar and Spice

SUGAR and spice and everything nice may be what proverbial little girls are made of, but the same formula applies to tasty appetizers, buffet casseroles, and all good food in general. Any kitchen from a one-burner hot plate to the magnificence of the block-long Americana kitchen ranges and work areas must have certain spices and flavoring agents no farther away than an arm's reach.

Two essential aids to savory appetizers are lemon juice and sour cream. These must be in every refrigerator, waiting their turn for that certain elusive something that turns spreads and dips into inspired eating.

The American Spice Trade Association has developed a splendid chart listing practically every known spice and where its particular flavor can be used at its best. Both chefs and potential cooks will be grateful for this spice chart, indicating compatible foods.

SPICE COMPATIBILITY CHART

NAME	DESCRIPTION	COMPATIBLE WITH
Allspice Spice	Whole Color—dried brown, pea-sized berries Flavor—spicy-sweet, mild, pleasant Ground Color—brown Flavor—same as above	Fruit compote, preserves, baked bananas; all cranberry dishes; spice cake, molasses cookies; spiced wine; beets, spinach, squash, turnips, red cabbage, carrots; green pea soup *; meat loaf, hamburgers, beef stew, baked ham, lamb, meat gravies *; mince meat; boiled fish *; pickles,* pickle-relishes; tapioca pudding, chocolate pudding

* Stars indicate that the whole spice can be used.

SPICE COMPATIBILITY CHART

NAME	DESCRIPTION	COMPATIBLE WITH
Anise Seed	Whole and Ground Color—brown with tan stripes Flavor—delightful sweet licorice aroma and taste	Coffee cake,* sweet bread rolls,* cookies *; fruit compote,* stewed apples,* preserved fruits,* all fruit pie fillings *; licorice candies; sweet pickles *; beef and veal stew *; cottage cheese
Barbecue Spice Blend	Color—reddish orange brown Flavor—piquant, with slight "smoky" overtone	Meats, poultry; fish; beans; in sauces for basting or cooking
Basil Herb	Available as dried crushed leaves and stems Color—light green Flavor—pleasant, mild, sweet, distinctive	All tomato dishes, peas, squash, string beans, potatoes, spinach; French and Russian dressings or sprinkle over salads; bean soup, pea soup, beef soup, Manhattan clam chowder; broiled lamb chops, venison, beef, lamb and veal stews, veal roasts; shrimp, shrimp creole, boiled and steamed lobster; spaghetti sauce; scrambled eggs; soufflés
Bay Leaves Herb	Available as dried whole leaves Color—light green Flavor—very mild, sweetly distinctive	Pickled beets, beets, boiled carrots, boiled artichokes, boiled potatoes; vegetable soup, fish chowders; lamb, beef, veal, venison, poultry, fish stews; boiled or steamed shrimp and lobster; chicken casserole, boiled chicken, pickled meats; brine for smoked meats; pot roast, boiled pork; meat gravies; marinades

SPICE COMPATIBILITY CHART

NAME	DESCRIPTION	COMPATIBLE WITH
Caraway Seed	Whole Color—dark brown with light brown stripes Flavor—tastes like rye bread; in fact, caraway gives rye bread its flavor	Mild cheese spreads, cream cheese, cottage cheese; bread, rolls, buns, muffins, coffee cake, cookies; cooked cabbage, cauliflower, potatoes, tomatoes, carrots, celery, onions, turnips, beets, broccoli, Brussels sprouts; cooked sauerkraut, coleslaw, salads; soup; sauerbraten, beef a la mode, roast pork, roast goose
Cardamom Seed	Whole and Ground Color—pod is cream colored, seeds dark brown Flavor—bittersweet, distinctive	Danish pastry, buns, coffee cake; grape jelly; custards; baked apple,* fruit cup, sprinkled on chilled melon; sweet potato dishes, pumpkin pie, cookies, frozen ice cream puddings
Cayenne Spice	Ground Color—burnt orange Flavor—hot	Deviled eggs; clam and oyster stews, poached salmon; seafood sauces, barbecue sauce for meat and fish; tuna fish salad; cottage and cream cheeses; cooked green vegetables; Welsh rarebit, cheese soufflés; pork chops, veal stew, ham croquettes
Celery Seed	Whole Color—deep to light shades of brownish-green Flavor—bitter celery	Cream of celery soup; meat loaf, meat stews; fish chowders and stews; celery sauce; coleslaw, pickles; cabbage, turnips, braised lettuce, white potatoes, stewed tomatoes; rolls, biscuits, salty bread; stuffings; eggs, salads and salad dressings

SPICE COMPATIBILITY CHART

NAME	DESCRIPTION	COMPATIBLE WITH
Celery Salt Vegetable Seasoning	Ground Color—grey beige Flavor—like celery heavily salted	Ham spread; chicken croquettes; boiled and fried eggs; cauliflower; potato salad; salad dressings; tomato and kraut juices; bouillon
Chili Powder Blend	Color—ranges from light to dark red Flavor—distinctive	Mexican cookery, arroz con pollo, chili con carne; meat loaf, hamburgers, beef, pork, veal stew; shellfish, creamed seafood; boiled and scrambled eggs; cocktail sauces; Spanish rice, gravies; pepperpot soup; vegetable relishes; French dressing
Cinnamon Spice	Whole Color—light brown Flavor—distinctive, sweet, spicy Ground Color—light brown Flavor—similar to above but sweeter and slightly stronger	Buns, coffee cake, muffins, spice cake, molasses cookies, butter cookies, cinnamon toast; custards, tapioca, chocolate pudding, rice pudding; fruit pies, broiled grapefruit, apples in any form, stewed fruits,* pickled fruits *; heated spiced beverages, hot cocoa and chocolate drinks; sweet gherkins; sweet potatoes, pumpkin, squash
Cloves Spice	Whole Color—dark brown Flavor—distinctive, spicy, sweet, penetrating Ground Color—rich brown Flavor—sharp, spicy, pungent	Ham,° boiled tongue,° pork roast *; pickled fruits,° preserved fruits,° stewed fruits *; apple, mince, and pumpkin pies; beets; baked beans; candied sweet potatoes; squash; hot spiced wines, hot tea; spice cake; sweet gherkins *; rice pudding; chocolate pudding; tapioca; bean soup; beef soup; cream of pea soup; cream of tomato soup

SPICE COMPATIBILITY CHART

NAME	DESCRIPTION	COMPATIBLE WITH
Crushed Red Pepper Spice	Color—bright red to orange Flavor—hot	Pizzas; sausages; Italian specialties; wherever heat or spot color is desired
Cumin Seed	Ground Color—gold with a hint of green Flavor—distinctive, salty-sweet, a principal flavoring ingredient of chili powder	Deviled eggs; cream, cottage and Cheddar cheeses *; meat loaf, hamburgers, chili con carne; fruit pies; cabbage,* rice; sauerkraut; fish
Curry Powder Blend	Color—varies depending on ingredients, predominantly rich gold Flavor—distinctive, exotic, with meat depending on blend	Eggs, deviled eggs; fish; shrimp; poultry, chicken hash; meat; vegetables, rice, scalloped tomatoes, creamed vegetables; cottage and cream cheeses; French dressing, mayonnaise, white sauce; clam and fish chowders; tomato soup, cream of mushroom soup; salted nuts; sweet pickles
Dill Seed	Whole Color—dark purplish brown with tan stripes Flavor—similar to caraway, but milder and sweeter Ground Color—tan Flavor—same as above	Pickling *; sauerkraut; potato salad; macaroni; cottage and cream cheeses; split pea soup, navy bean soup, cream of tomato soup; apple pie; broiled lamb chops, lamb stew; creamed chicken; French dressing, sour cream salad dressing; drawn butter for shellfish; spiced vinegar; peas, carrots, beets, cabbage, cauliflower, snap beans, turnips
Fennel Seed	Whole Color—light sand-colored seed with brown stripes Flavor—sweet licorice, mild, anise-like	Sweet pickles; boiled fish; bread, buns, coffee cake, muffins, sugar cookies; apples in any form; beef stew; squash; roast pork

SPICE COMPATIBILITY CHART

NAME	DESCRIPTION	COMPATIBLE WITH
Garlic Powder Vegetable Seasoning	Color—white Flavor—garlic (product is result of dehydrating and grinding garlic) Contains no salt Granulated garlic is similar product but more coarsely ground	Wherever garlic is used
Garlic Salt Vegetable Seasoning	Color—white Flavor—similar to garlic powder but much milder because of addition of salt	Wherever slight garlic flavor is desired
Ginger Spice	Whole Color—tan Flavor—distinctive, spicy, penetrating Ground Color—light tan Flavor—same as above	Cookies, spice cake, pumpkin pie; Indian pudding; baked, stewed and preserved fruits; apple sauce; custard; conserves; chutney, buttered beets; carrots; squash; poultry; broiled and chopped beef, lamb and veal; bean soup; pickles; baked beans; cheese dishes; meat stews; French dressing
Instant Minced Onion Vegetable Seasoning	Dehydrated minced Color—white Flavor—real onion flavor	Wherever minced or finely chopped onion is used
Mace Spice	Whole Color—burnt orange Flavor—sweet exotic aroma and strong nutmeg flavor Ground Color—gold	Fish sauces,* oyster and clam stews; creamed soups; pickling,* preserved fruits,* gingerbread batter; stewed cherries,* fruit salad *; sweet spiced doughs, doughnuts, light fruit cakes, pound cake; Welsh rarebit *; meat loaf,

SPICE COMPATIBILITY CHART

NAME	DESCRIPTION	COMPATIBLE WITH
Mace Spice	Flavor—same as above	veal chops; all chocolate dishes; whipped cream; cottage pudding, custard; carrots, cauliflower, potatoes, spinach, succotash; fruit pies
Marjoram Herb	Whole and Ground Color—green Flavor—distinctive, delicate	Lamb chops, roast beef, pork, veal, chicken, duck, goose; salmon loaf and other baked and broiled fish; omelets and soufflés; tossed green salad; onion, clam and oyster soups; stews, eggplants, carrots, peas, spinach; stuffings
Mint Herb	Whole Color—green Flavor—distinctive, sweet aroma Flaked Color—green Flavor—same as above	Jelly, ice cream, custard, fruit salad, fruit compote; frostings; split pea soup; lamb and veal roast sauces; cottage cheese salad; white potatoes, cabbage, carrots, celery, snap beans; tea; mint sauce

Mixed
Pickling
Spice
Blend of
Whole
Spices
	Flavor—in cooking,
	  blend is distinctive,
	  pleasant, spicy and
	  sweet
		Pickles, relishes; preserves; gravies; meat stews, pork, veal, lamb, beef; cooked vegetables; boiled salmon; marinades; shrimp

Mustard
Seed
	Whole
	Color—light to
	  dark brown
	Flavor—distinctive,
	  spicy, sharp
	Powdered
	Color—light yellow
	Flavor—distinctive,
	  spicy, sharp
		Pickles,* pickled onions *; salads,* salad dressings; pickled meats *; boiled fish *; Chinese hot sauce, fish sauces, cheese sauces; ham, kidneys; deviled eggs; creamed and stewed oysters, shrimp; asparagus, beets, broccoli, Brussels sprouts, cabbage, celery, onions, white potatoes, snap beans, squash; molasses cookies; hot English mustard, prepared mustard

SPICE COMPATIBILITY CHART

NAME	DESCRIPTION	COMPATIBLE WITH
Nutmeg Spice	Ground Color—copper Flavor—distinctive, exotic, sweet	Doughnuts; eggnog, custards, puddings, whipped cream, ice cream; fried bananas, stewed fruits; spice cake, coffee cake, cookies, pumpkin pie; steamed and glazed carrots, cabbage, spinach, snap beans, squash, onions, sweet potatoes; meat loaf
Onion Powder Vegetable Seasoning	Color—white Flavor—onion (product is result of dehydrating and grinding onion) Contains no salt Granulated onion is similar product but more coarsely ground	Wherever onion flavor is desired
Onion Salt Vegetable Seasoning	Color—cream Flavor—similar to onion powder but much milder because of addition of salt	Wherever slight onion flavor is desired
Oregano Herb	Whole Color—green Flavor—distinctive, strong Ground Color—olive green Flavor—same as above	Pizza pie, spaghetti sauce, meat sauce; Swiss steak, beef stew, broiled and roast lamb, pork and veal, poultry; gravies; stuffed fish; cheese spreads; beef soup, bean soup, tomato soup; butter sauce for shellfish; cream and tomato sauces; vegetable juice cocktail; onions, peas, white potatoes, spinach, string beans

SPICE COMPATIBILITY CHART

NAME	DESCRIPTION	COMPATIBLE WITH
Paprika Spice	Ground Color—red Flavor—distinctive, very mild	Poultry, ham, goulash, fish, shellfish; salad dressings; vegetables, gravies; cheese, Welsh rarebit; canapés; deviled eggs; stuffed celery, cream soups, chicken soup, chowders
Parsley Flakes Herb	Color—green Flavor—distinctive, mild	Soups; salads; coleslaw; meat, stews, fish, poultry; sauces; all vegetables; omelets; potatoes
Black Pepper Spice	Whole Color—dark brown Flavor—distinctive, pleasant spicy bouquet with palate-tingling flavor and enduring aftertaste Ground Color—varies from cream to black Flavor—same as above	Almost all foods, except those with sweet flavors. If you are preparing a nonsweet dish that "needs something" try a little pepper first. It is used universally to add sparkle to foods, including: pickles *; soups *; poultry, meats,* fish,* shellfish, game; sauces, gravies, marinades; salads; eggs; cheese spreads; vegetables; spiced vinegar
White Pepper Spice	Whole Color—varies from beige to brown Flavor—penetrating, strong with enduring aftertaste Ground Color—light sand Flavor—same as above	Same as above. White pepper is used where black specks are not desired, such as in white sauces, clear soups, mashed potatoes, etc.
Poppy Seed	Whole Color—predominantly blue-gray Flavor—crunchy texture, nutlike	Breads, rolls, coffee cake, cookies, pie crusts; noodles; cottage cheese; salad dressing; green peas, white potatoes, rutabagas

SPICE COMPATIBILITY CHART

NAME	DESCRIPTION	COMPATIBLE WITH
Rosemary Herb	Whole Color—green (looks like a pine needle) Flavor—distinctive, delicate, sweetish	Roast and broiled lamb, beef, pork, veal, game, poultry; salmon; deviled eggs; cheese sauces; sautéed mushrooms, boiled potatoes, green peas, squash; creamed seafood; chicken soup, split pea soup
Sage Herb	Whole Color—olive green Flavor—distinctive, positive	All pork dishes, meat, fish and poultry stuffings; brown sauces; cheese spreads; consommé, cream soups, fish chowders; salad greens, French dressing; Brussels sprouts, onions, lima beans, peas, tomatoes
Saffron Spice	Whole and Ground Color—predominantly maroon Flavor—distinctive, exotic, concentrated (not strong, yet a little goes a long way)	Rice; rolls, breads, buns; fish stew; bouillabaise chicken; chicken soup; cakes
Savory Herb	Whole and Ground Color—green Flavor—distinctive, pleasant, mild	Scrambled eggs, omelets, deviled eggs; liver paste, chicken loaf, poultry, stuffing; hamburgers, lamb pie, veal roast, fish; tossed salad, lentil soup, consommé, fish chowder, beets, beans, cabbage, peas
Sesame Seed	Whole Color—predominantly cream Flavor—crunchy texture, sweet, decidedly nutlike	Rolls, breads, buns, cookies, coffee cake, pies; soft cheeses, salad dressings; fish; asparagus, snap beans, tomatoes; candies

SPICE COMPATIBILITY CHART

NAME	DESCRIPTION	COMPATIBLE WITH
Tarragon Herb	Whole and Ground Color—green Flavor—distinctive, fresh, pleasant	Marinades for meat, butter sauce for steaks; poultry; salads; omelets; fish and shellfish; vegetable juice cocktail; chicken soup, consommé, fish chowder, tomato soup; vinegar; broccoli, asparagus, beans, cabbage, cauliflower
Thyme Herb	Whole Color—gray-green Flavor—distinctive, pleasantly penetrating Ground Color—light olive green Flavor—slightly stronger than above	Fresh tomtatoes, tomato aspic, salads; poultry stuffing, croquettes, fricassees; fish chowders, gumbo, vegetable soup, shirred eggs; all meats; seafood sauces; artichokes, beans, beets, carrots, mushrooms, onions, potatoes
Turmeric Spice	Whole and Ground Color—orange (used mostly for its color) Flavor—mild, slightly bitter	Pickles, relishes, prepared mustards, salad dressings; creamed eggs, fish, seafood; to color rice dishes where saffron is not used

12. Equipment

chafing dishes
silver serving platters
French knife
paring knife *
channel knife *
boning knife *
cook's knife *
poultry shears *
lobster shears *
beef slicer *
kitchen fork *
tomato knife *
grapefruit knife *
ball cutter *
household steel *
larding and vegetable knife *
scallop knife *
vegetable peeler
slicer, roast
parisienne knife
fancy timbales
truffle cutters

brochettes (skewer)
cheese grater
measuring cup
stainless steel mixing bowls (various sizes)
pastry bag (with various star tubes)
pastry brush
spatula
frilled toothpicks
paper frills or stockings
doilies (assorted sizes and colors)
casseroles (metal and crockery, assorted sizes and shapes)
molds (copper, aluminum, and glass, assorted sizes and shapes)
cookie cutters (assorted)
roasting and baking pans
deep fat fryer
ice cream scoop (no. 30 or no. 40)
cookie sheets
various size pots and pans (metal)
strainers or china caps
cheesecloth

* See illustration.

153

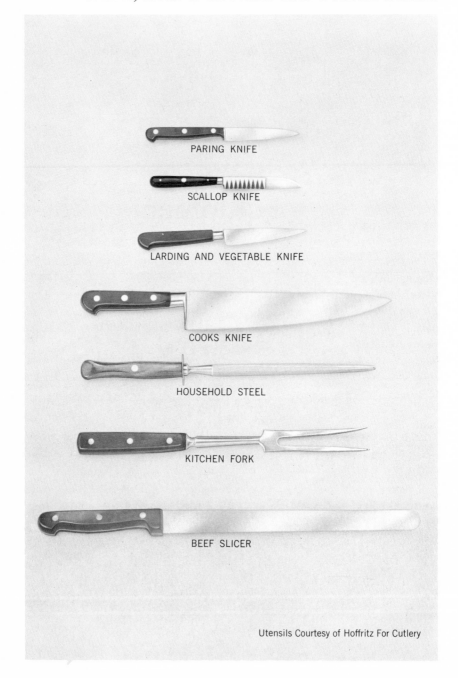

PARING KNIFE

SCALLOP KNIFE

LARDING AND VEGETABLE KNIFE

COOKS KNIFE

HOUSEHOLD STEEL

KITCHEN FORK

BEEF SLICER

Utensils Courtesy of Hoffritz For Cutlery

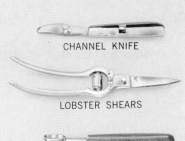

CHANNEL KNIFE

LOBSTER SHEARS

MELON-BALL CUTTER

GRAPEFRUIT KNIFE

TOMATO KNIFE

POULTRY SHEARS

BONING KNIFE

13. From the Grocers' Shelf

smoked oysters, clams, and eels
smoked salmon in jars
truffled foie gras
smoked turkey and turkey pâté
pickled sausages
pickled mushrooms, onions, and various vegetables
all varieties of stuffed olives
Italian antipasto in jars
canned artichoke hearts
canned anchovies, sardines, tuna
caviar
smoked salmon, sturgeon, and whitefish from the specialty grocer
herring, rollmops, and tidbits in cream or wine sauce
frozen fried shrimp, scallops, and fish sticks
frozen pizzas
frozen miniatures of knishes, meat balls, and pigs in blankets
chicken, liver, deviled ham, and corned beef spreads in cans
canned meat balls and fish balls
every type of cheese
fresh cheese dips and spreads from the dairy food counter

Just browse in any food shop and keep an open mind. The treasures you will find will amaze you.

14. Tables of Cost Breakdown

The Food Service Department of Sexton Quality Foods has developed a cost per service chart that should prove of value to anyone —amateur or professional, who wishes to start or build up a cocktail hour or private catering business. Through the kind permission of Sexton's the following tables are made available.

SUGGESTED RELISHES

ITEM	ALLOWANCE PER PERSON	COST PER PERSON
Vegetables		
Radish Roses	2	$ .010
Celery Sticks	2	.015
Stuffed Celery Hearts	2	.025
Carrot Sticks	2	.005
Carrot Curls	3-4	.005
Green Onions	1	.010
Pickled Rosebud Beets	2	.015
Marinated Tiny Whole Onions	2	.020
Pickles and Olives		
Ripe Olives (Giant)	2	.020
Green Olives, plain (Large)	2	.030
Green Olives, stuffed (Large)	2	.030
Sweet Pickle Chips	3	.015
Home Style Pickle Quarters	2	.025
Cantaloupe Cubes, Preserved	2	.030
Watermelon Cubes	2	.030
Sweet Gherkins (Midget)	2	.030
Sweet Mixed Pickles		.025
Relishes		
Corn Relish	1 oz.	.025
Pepper Relish	1 oz.	.030
Chow Relish	1½ oz.	.025
Cottage Cheese with chives	1½ oz.	.020

RELISH COMBINATIONS

DESCRIPTION	COST PER PERSON

Number 1

Radish Roses
Celery Sticks
Ripe Olives
Sweet Pickle Chips
Watermelon Cubes
Corn Relish $. 11

Number 2

Green Onions
Stuffed Celery Hearts
Pickled Beets
Stuffed Green Olives
Cottage Cheese with chives $ .10

Number 3

Carrot Sticks
Tiny Whole Onions
Ripe Olives
Sweet Mixed Pickles
Chow Relish $ .09

Number 4

Green Onions
Pickled Rosebud Beets
Plain Green Olives
Home Style Pickle Quarters
Red Pepper Relish $ .10

Number 5

Radish Roses
Carrot Curls
Green Onions

RELISH COMBINATIONS

DESCRIPTION	COST PER PERSON

Number 5 (cont'd)

    Watermelon Cubes
    Ripe Olives
    Sweet Pickle Chips $ .10

Number 6

    Radish Roses
    Stuffed Celery Hearts
    Ripe Olives
    Home Style Pickle Quarters
    Cottage Cheese with chives $ .10

Number 7

    Radish Roses
    Stuffed Celery Hearts
    Green Onions
    Carrot Curls
    Pickled Rosebud Beets $ .07

Number 8

    Ripe Olives
    Stuffed Queen Olives
    Cantaloupe Cubes
    Home Style Pickle Quarters
    Midget Sweet Gherkins $ .13

Number 9

    Sweet Mixed Pickles
    Corn Relish
    Pepper Relish
    Chow Relish
    Cottage Cheese with chives $ .12

HORS D'OEUVRES SUGGESTIONS

Canapé Spreads

Anchovy Paste	Pate Maison	Salmon Paste
Sardine Paste	Lobster Paste	Deviled Ham
Shrimp Paste	Avocado Spread	Spiced Cheese
Cream Cheese	Caviar	Chicken Liver
(flavored)	Chicken Salad	and Bacon
Smoked Salmon Paste	Deviled Egg Spread	Deviled Clam

The above canapé spreads are all of a nature that they go a long way, and can be used to produce canapés at a reasonable cost. Including the toast shapes and/or crackers, they can be produced for less than fifty cents a dozen, raw food cost.

	ALLOWANCE PER PERSON	COST PER PERSON
Savories		
Medium Shrimp	2-3	$ .10-.15
Rolled Filets of Anchovies with capers	3-4	.05-.06
Marinated Mushrooms (Medium Buttons)	3-4	.04-.05
Smoked Oysters	3-4	.03-.04
Smoked Clams	3-4	.03-.04
Marinated Herring in Cream	2-3	.10-.15
Cream or Sharp Cheese Balls	2-3	.06-.09
Sharp Cheese Cubes	2-3	.02-.03
Marinated Tiny Whole Onions	2-3	.02-.03
Marinated Rosebud Beets	2-3	.02-.03
Cocktail Franks	2-3	.04-.06

The allowance per person above is predicated on an assortment of four or five different items in the assortment. These four or five items may be divided between the canapés and the savories for a cold hors d'oeuvres tray.

	ALLOWANCE PER PERSON	COST PER PERSON
Hot Hors D'Oeuvres		
Cocktail Franks	2-3	$ .04-.06
Cocktail Salami Sausages	2-3	.04-.06
Cocktail Meatballs	3-4	.05-.06
Broiled Mushrooms (Large Caps)	2-3	.08-.12
Broiled Boneless Sardines	2-3	.09-.13

HORS D'OEUVRES SUGGESTIONS

	ALLOWANCE PER PERSON	COST PER PERSON
Miscellaneous		
Antipasto		$ .10-.20
Flat Filets of Anchovies		.04-.06
Deviled Eggs	1-2	.03-.06

COCKTAIL PARTY COMBINATIONS

Deluxe Assortment (Cost: 45-50 cents per person)

Assorted Canapés (Allowance: 3 each)
Anchovy Paste, Cream Cheese and Caviar, Avocado Spread
Assorted Savories (Allowance: 3 each)
Medium Shrimp, Smoked Oysters, Cream Cheese Balls
Cocktail Salamis, Cocktail Meatballs (Allowance: 3 each)

Deluxe Assortment (Cost: 35-40 cents per person)

Assorted Canapés
Shrimp Paste, Chicken Salad Spread, Spiced Cheese Spread
Assorted Savories
Rolled Filets of Anchovies with capers, Marinated Mushrooms, Sharp Cheese Cubes
Cocktail Franks
Broiled Boneless Sardines

Medium Assortment (Cost: 30-35 cents per person)

Assorted Canapés
Deviled Eggs Spread, Chicken Liver and Bacon, Cream Cheese and Olive Spread
Assorted Savories
Marinated Rosebud Beets, Smoked Clams, Sharp Cheese Cubes
Cocktail Franks
Broiled Mushrooms

COCKTAIL PARTY COMBINATIONS

Medium Assortment (Cost: 30-35 cents per person)

Assorted Canapés
   Sardine Paste, Pate Maison, Deviled Ham
Assorted Savories
   Rolled Filets of Anchovies with capers, Smoked Oysters, Marinated Whole
   Onions
Cocktail Meatballs
   Broiled Mushrooms

Economy Assortment (Cost: 20-25 cents per person)

Assorted Canapés
   Lobster Paste, Spiced Cheese, Deviled Egg Spread
Assorted Savories
   Marinated Mushrooms, Cream Cheese Balls
Cocktail Meatballs or Cocktail Salamis

Economy Assortment (Cost: 20-25 cents per person)

Assorted Canapés
   Anchovy Paste, Deviled Clam Spread
Assorted Savories
   Marinated Mushrooms, Smoked Clams, Sharp Cheese Cubes
Broiled Boneless Sardines or Cocktail Salamis

Index